JEWS,

TURKS,

AND

INFIDELS

JEWS,

TURKS,

AND

INFIDELS

MORTON BORDEN

The University of North Carolina Press

Chapel Hill and London

© 1984 The University of North Carolina Press

Manufactured in the United States of America

Library of Congress Cataloging in Publication Data

Borden, Morton.
  Jews, Turks, and infidels.

  Bibliography: p.
  1. Jews—Legal status, laws, etc.—United States.
2. Religious liberty—United States.   3. Jews—United
States—Politics and government.   4. United States—
Politics and government—19th century.   5. United
States—Ethnic relations.   I. Title.
E184.J5B68   1984   323.44'2'0973   83-19863
ISBN 0-8078-1592-6

Portions of this work have appeared in somewhat
different form in *Civil War History* 25, no. 2 (June 1979)
and *Journal of Church and State* 21 (Autumn 1979).

CONTENTS

ACKNOWLEDGMENTS

I am in considerable debt to several of my colleagues in the Department of History at the University of California, Santa Barbara, who read and made corrective suggestions as this manuscript took form; and I am particularly grateful to my wife, Penn, not only for her patience in listening to my tiresome lectures on the subject of Jews in America—without demanding equal time for Norwegians in America—but for her intelligent and perceptive comments. This book is dedicated to her.

Religious liberty and political liberty shared the same umbilical cord of the American Revolution. One could not survive without the other, and both were nurtured on a rich prenatal diet of supporting declarations. Foreign soldiers who fought for the English monarch, for example, were promised protection "in the free exercise of their respective religions" if they would defect to the rebel side. Patrick Henry drafted that part of the Virginia Declaration of Rights in 1776 which stated that "all men are equally entitled to the free exercise of religion." As colonies became states, most adopted bills of rights that guaranteed freedom of religion. So did the federal government.

At the same time, many Americans defined the United States as a Christian nation. Jews, Turks, and Infidels (or any other exotic group), they believed, could worship as they pleased but had no right to participate in its government. Some of the same state constitutions that guaranteed religious liberty also contained provisions that restricted holding office to Christians or to Protestants. In several states those restrictions were defended and maintained well into the nineteenth century. The Constitution of the United States, to be sure, recognized no religious distinctions of any kind; but that applied to federal, not state, offices. Moreover, the Constitution was subject to judicial interpretation and to political amendment. Did the Constitution permit blasphemy prosecutions? Sunday laws? To what extent, if any, did common-law protections of Christianity apply under the Constitution? In short, what would America be: secular or Christian? Both messages were broadcast simultaneously. Obviously there was a gap between the rhetoric of religious liberty and the fact of religious bigotry; between the will of what some Christians claimed to be the opinion of the majority and the rights of the minority.

The expansion of religious liberty (and its political sibling) was not an inevitable result of the Revolution, or even of the Constitution, though many scholars so argue. It did not come easily, and it did not simply ripen and fall to non-Christians as a gift of the Protestant majority. Religious liberty had to be fought for in legislative halls, constitutional conventions, and in state and federal courts. Not only were there discriminatory state laws to be eradicated, but federal practices had to be monitored constantly lest the Constitution be converted into a Christian document. Especially in the nineteenth century a resurgent and imperial Protestantism attempted to subvert what gains had been achieved. Though few in number, unorganized, with their membership seduced by secularism, and against the advice of those who counseled silence or compromise, certain Jewish leaders insisted upon equality before the law. The Jewish presence in America and its vigilance were significant factors in broadening the definition of religious liberty.

JEWS,

TURKS,

AND

INFIDELS

O N E

No State Shall Violate the Equal Rights of Conscience

*The scholarly literature explaining the religious be-
liefs of Americans in the early national period is as
varied as was the population and as contradictory as
were their motives. It is said, for example, that only a
small percentage of the people attended any church,
that they were largely apathetic about religion, and
that even in Virginia "those who fought the establishment . . . were often so lackadaisical that they had to
be coached and even provided with sectarian names
when they came to register their dissent."[1] Such was
indeed the case in certain areas and circumstances,
but in Virginia and elsewhere passions ran high
on the issue of extending religious liberty to non-
Christians or non-Protestants. Another scholar notes
that the authors of the Constitution were philosophi-
cally committed to freedom of religion: "These men
. . . were convinced that the emerging Federal government should have no connection with any Church,
and that religious freedom should prevail."[2] Again,
this statement is only partly true: A number of the
founding fathers fought to maintain the privileged
status of particular churches within their respective
states. Finally, the attitudes of those who opposed the
Constitution, the Anti-Federalists, is especially puz-
zling. On one hand, they insisted upon a bill of rights
that would include a guarantee of religious freedom;
on the other hand, many criticized the Constitution*

*for its failure to provide a Protestant test oath for
federal office. Scholars generally conclude that these
Anti-Federalists were motivated by intolerance.*[3] *Yet,
if that is so, why did an impressive number of Anti-
Federalist essayists ignore Article 6, section 3, while
attacking other parts of the Constitution? It was an
obvious target, an easy provision to denounce, had
they been so inclined.*

*Viewing this period from a Jewish perspective
serves to enlighten our understanding of these questions. Jews feared the potential of Protestant unity.
They were alert to the discriminations contained in
the state constitutions, and thus to the liberating significance of Article 6, section 3, of the federal
Constitution.*

A Philadelphia Parade

The memory of an old Jewish gentleman, Naphtali
Phillips, was extraordinarily accurate at age ninety-five. He could look
back over eight decades and still recall the parade of 4 July 1788 in
Philadelphia, which celebrated both the anniversary of the Declaration
of Independence and Virginia's recent ratification of the Constitution.
He remembered Chief Justice Thomas McKean, who sat in an open
carriage, holding the new Constitution, and the applause of the crowd.
There was a float honoring agriculture, which carried cattle and sheep,
with farmers walking beside it strewing grain; another with a live forge
worked with a huge bellows, the flame symbolizing liberty; another
featured a printing press, with the compositors setting type and jour-
neymen passing out printed matter; another was the replica of a ship
that bore young mariners singing "By the Deep Nine," "Quarter Less
Seven," and other sailor songs; and three "fine-looking" men dressed
in black velvet and elegant powdered wigs represented the hairdress-
ing society. Phillips could not recall all of the parade or its exact order.
And how could he? There were, according to contemporary accounts,
eighty-six parts to it, which included the consuls of foreign countries,
judges, military officers, and representatives of every conceivable oc-

cupational and professional group in the city. It was over a mile in length and took an entire morning to pass in review. At its conclusion there was an open-air banquet set on "a very large circular range of tables, covered with canvas awnings, and plentifully spread with a cold collation," as one newspaper reported. Phillips remembered this feast, because care had been taken to prepare a separate table with special foods that the Jewish citizens of Philadelphia could eat without violating their dietary laws.[4]

Strangely, Phillips did not mention one part of the parade that struck another observer as particularly appropriate. In eighty-fourth place—after the "gentlemen of the bar" but before "the college of physicians"—marched seventeen clergymen. They "formed a very agreeable part of the procession," Benjamin Rush noted. "Pains were taken to connect Ministers of the most dissimilar religious principles together, thereby to show the influence of a free government in promoting christian charity. The Rabbi of the Jews, locked in the arms of two ministers of the gospel, was a most delightful sight. There could not have been a more happy emblem contrived, which opens all its power and offices alike, not only to every sect of christians, but to worthy men of *every* religion."[5]

Such a scene was truly remarkable for the year 1788. It could not have been duplicated anywhere else in the Western world, including many parts of America. The clerical linking of arms had real meaning for Jews—indeed, for all religious minorities—because it was fortified by the Constitution, which expressly barred any religious conditions for federal officeholding. Article 6, section 3, stated that "no religious test shall ever be required as a qualification to any office or public trust under the United States." This provision was much more significant to Jews than the Bill of Rights, which was passed a few years later, and with good reason. One could find handsomely phrased generalities about religious freedom in many of the state constitutions, yet these same states, with little sense of contradiction, barred either non-Christians or non-Protestants from holding office. What good were constitutional declarations without substance? Article 6, section 3, meant equality, at least on the federal level, which made the attainment of religious liberty possible.

By 1788 Jews had, in a word, achieved toleration in the United States. None of the state governments threatened the "free" exercise of religion. What Jews now sought was equality, which the federal

Constitution guaranteed, but which many of the state constitutions specifically denied.

The Pressures to Convert

Statistically the number of Jews in America at the time that the Constitution was ratified was insignificant, somewhere between 1,500 and 2,000.[6] These few were concentrated in five "urban" centers—New York, Philadelphia, Newport, Charleston, and Savannah—outside of which most Americans never encountered a Jew, except occasionally in the occupation of an itinerant peddler. As one might expect, attitudes towards Jews varied considerably, forming a curious amalgam of respect and prejudice that has remained constant throughout American history. There was prejudice, of course. Some, who had absorbed centuries of European anti-Semitic thought, hated Jews as a people who denied Christ, and they suspected them of sharp dealings and strange rituals. But there was respect as well. Some revered Jews as descendants of Old Testament figures, as if they were living fossils whose preservation and study might reveal Hebraic truths that in turn would lead to a better comprehension of the Bible.[7]

Cases of individuals experiencing sudden and dramatic shifts between these extremes have been well documented. The Reverend Ezra Stiles of Rhode Island, for example, initially referred to Jews as an obdurate and unassimilable people. Despite their colonial residence, which had extended over a century, he predicted that Jews "will never become incorporated with the People of America any more than in Europe, Asia, and Africa." Later Stiles befriended a number of Jews, relishing an exchange of theological scholarship with them. "I have been taught personally at the mouths of the Masters of Wisdom," he told an audience at Yale in 1781, "at [the] mouths of five Rabbis, Hochams [learned men] of names and Eminence." Still, when a Jewish friend died, Stiles's main regret was that the deceased never "perceived the Truth . . . that JESUS was the MESSIAH predicted by Moses and the Prophets!"[8]

The pressures on Jews to convert to Protestantism were enormous. Naturally, as in Europe, the stigma of conversion was always present, but a convert immediately possessed the full rights of citizenship, which were denied to Jews; moreover, his children or grandchildren became indistinguishable from the Protestant mass. In 1784 the Reverend Charles Crawford reprinted an old tract by George Fox, *A Looking-Glass for the Jews*, with a preface that advised Christians to exhibit a greater tolerance of Jews, for this "has a tendency to bring them over to the gospel, and therefore the unlimited toleration of them is the cause of God."[9] Few Protestant evangelists followed Crawford's advice, and Jews recognized the fundamental anti-Semitism of most missionaries. By 1816 a formal organization, The American Society for Evangelizing the Jews, supported by some 200 local auxiliaries and with a roster of distinguished Americans as its officers, financed the work of Protestant missionaries among the Jews. That organization was followed by many others. All were spectacularly unsuccessful. Timothy Dwight, president of Yale College, commented that "several Jews have indeed embraced Christianity in this country [New England], as well as elsewhere," but rarely were their conversions sincere. He referred to one "very uncommon, if not a singular instance" of conversion, a uniqueness acknowledged by Christians and Jews: "the Christians by their general respect for him, and the Jews by their hatred and obloquy."[10] Half a century later, in 1871, a Philadelphia newspaper calculated that missionary activities to the Jews "shows a miserable return . . . the conversion of a sixth of a Jew per annum."[11] A recent scholar has noted that "missionaries actually posed only a petty threat to American Jewry. They continued to ply their trade, and American Jewry continued to battle them. But outsiders knew that widespread conversion would never take place. Eight decades of struggle had sensitized Jews to their own identities and past history."[12]

If conversions to Protestantism were comparatively rare, yet another more insidious form of assimilation also enticed Jews to abandon their faith: the secularity that long coexisted with Protestantism at the core of the American experience.[13] Many succumbed to it, but Jews who did not were caught between the opposing pillars of Protestantism and secularism, sometimes with odd results. The artist John Trumbull recalled being invited to a dinner party at the home of Thomas Jefferson in 1793, at which "a discussion of the Christian religion ensued." Christianity, he reported, was "powerfully ridiculed on the one side, and weakly defended on the other." It was "a rather freethinking dinner party." One guest, William Branch Giles, "proceeded so far at last, as to ridicule the character, conduct, and doctrines of the divine founder of our religion." Jefferson listened, "smiling and nodding approbation on Mr. Giles." A Jewish guest, David Franks—at the time first cashier of the Bank of the United States—disturbed by the vehemence of Giles's remarks, argued in favor of Trumbull, who was a devout Congregationalist. Trumbull was so struck by this that he remarked to Jefferson, "Sir, this is a strange situation in which I find myself; in a country professing Christianity, and at a table with Christians, as I supposed, I find my religion and myself attacked with severe and almost irresistible wit and raillery, and not a person to aid me in my defense, but my friend Mr. Franks, *who is himself a Jew*." [14]

Christian Views and Jewish Fears

From 1776 on, conflicts over religious liberty—its definition, extent, and precise application—agitated society in many states. Except for presenting a few random petitions to state legislatures reminding the lawmakers of their revolutionary war services and praying that they be granted political equality, Jews did not, indeed, could not participate in these debates. They were largely bystanders, powerless to affect the result. Who spoke for them? Who supported, even indirectly, their quest for equality?

Certainly not other religious minorities. They were concerned exclusively with the acquisition of political rights for themselves. Isaac Backus, for example, the famous Baptist leader in Massachusetts, wrote stinging attacks against ecclesiastical establishments and is usually cited for the pronounced emphasis of his arguments in favor of separation of church and state. One of his last pamphlets, however, entitled *A Door Opened for Equal Christian Liberty* (1783), exalted the emerging Christian (not secular) state. "No man," he commented with approval, "can take a seat in our [state] legislature till he solemnly declares, 'I believe the Christian religion and have a firm persuasion of its truth.'" [15] The Roman Catholic bishop, John Carroll of Maryland, advised Catholics to conduct their ecclesiastical affairs so as to maintain "equal civil rights with other Christians." In an essay written anonymously for *The Columbian Magazine* in 1787, Carroll thanked "the genuine spirit of Christianity" by which several states "have done . . . justice to every denomination of christians, which ought to be done to them in all, of placing them on the same footing of citizenship, and conferring an equal right of participation in national privileges. Freedom and independence, acquired by the united efforts, and cemented with the mingled blood of protestant and catholic fellow-citizens, should be equally enjoyed by all."[16] Carroll's strategy was to maintain theological distinctions between Catholic and Protestant, yet to fuse them politically. If the visions of Backus or Carroll had prevailed, American Jews would have remained second-class citizens.

Jewish apprehensions that they would be denied equality were based on the real possibility of an ecumenical Protestantism or Christianity, especially the former, being constitutionally recognized on the national level as it already was in several states. In 1790 some sixty-two percent of American churches were in substantial agreement on the fundamentals of Calvinism. The logic of those who thought of America as a Protestant nation ran somewhat as follows:

1. The civil order and the spiritual order are interrelated and interdependent.
2. If Protestantism, in all its forms, is the true faith, then those who deny it are wrong.
3. If Jews and other non-Protestants are to be tolerated, still they should not be allowed to govern.
4. Government, to remain strong and virtuous, must be allied to the religion of the majority.

Some of the most radical pamphleteers of the American revolution so argued. The anonymous author of *The People the Best Governors; Or A Plan of Government Founded on the Just Principles of Natural Freedom* (1776), declared that no property qualifications whatsoever should be imposed for holding office, and that all white males should possess the suffrage. But he also recommended "that no person shall be capable of holding any public office except he possesses a belief of one only invisible God, that governs all things; and that the Bible is his revealed word; and that he be also an honest, moral man."[17] In that same year Samuel Adams advised Americans to inaugurate a "reign of political Protestantism." Protestantism and liberty were indivisible, another essayist argued. It was the religion most conducive "to Industry, Commerce, the Arts, Science, Freedom, and [the] consequent temporal Happiness of Mankind." It was the religion "of the greatest, wisest, and best men this world has ever produced." Government must "honor" Protestantism by affording it "every possible distinguishing mark of preeminence."[18]

Jewish hopes for obtaining equality, on the other hand, depended upon two complementary factors. *First*, among the educated classes of America, the cult of reason was widespread. Few of these persons were overtly anticlerical, as were so many leaders of the French Enlightenment. Christianity must be cleansed of its superstitions, Jefferson argued. "The day will come," he wrote to John Adams, "when the mystical generation of Jesus, by the supreme being as his father in the womb of a virgin will be classed with the fable of the generation of Minerva in the brain of Jupiter."[19] Jefferson had a particular distaste for Calvinist doctrine and its bigoted practitioners. Nevertheless, men like Jefferson and Franklin believed that churches of every denomination were an effective institution for the social control of the common people. "Talking against religion," Franklin warned, "is unchaining a tiger; the beast let loose may worry his liberator."[20] All religion was to be encouraged. All had merit. But the principles that religion was a private concern, that Christianity or Protestantism had no monopoly of truth, that government must be divorced from religion, neither favoring nor discriminating, had taken firm hold, at least among the intellectual elite. Such views probably represented a minority opinion of the general public. Thus it is rather ironic that Jewish hopes for equality rested in part with spokesmen whose outlook was secular and rationalist, closet skeptics whose indifference to the supremacy of any one faith permitted them to champion religious liberty for all. *Second*, despite the Calvinist majority, Jews hoped that instead of an ecumenical Protestantism expressed politically, precisely the opposite would occur: Out of mutual suspicions and competitive fears, the multiplicity of Protestant groups would support religious liberty as a matter of pragmatic necessity.

At Philadelphia, in 1787, as we know, the combination of principle and necessity proved irresistible. Article 6, section 3, was the result. But that result was neither assured nor inevitable. It came about after a dozen years of debate. Instead of religious liberty for all, America might have become a nation governed only by Protestants who tolerated others but rejected their quest for equality.

The First State Constitutions

In North Carolina, in 1776, for example, a Presbyterian divine, the Reverend David Caldwell, insisted upon the inclusion of a provision in the state constitution whereby "no person, who shall deny the being of God or the truth of the Protestant religion, or the divine authority of the Old or New Testaments, or who shall hold religious principles incompatible with the freedom and safety of the State, shall be capable of holding any office or place of trust or profit in the civil department within this State." Governor Samuel Johnston was firmly opposed to such a provision but, as he informed James Iredell, it "was carried after a very warm debate, and has blown up such a flame, that everything is in danger of being thrown into confusion."[21]

A similar conflict took place in Pennsylvania that same year, although the proposed ban on holding office was limited to Jews and atheists and referred specifically to seats in the legislature. Benjamin Franklin, who presided at the state convention, wanted no religious test whatsoever. But "being overpowered by Numbers," he explained to Joseph Priestley, "and fearing more [restrictions] might in future Times be grafted on it, I prevailed to have the additional clause '*that no further or more extended Profession of Faith shall ever be exacted.*'"[22] The Reverend Henry Muhlenberg, senior minister of the German Lutheran congregation in Pennsylvania, objected bitterly. He wanted the restrictions to be broader both in definition and in application. "It now seems," Muhlenberg remarked, "as if a Christian people were [to be] ruled by Jews, Turks, Spinozists, Deists, [and] perverted naturalists." An anonymous contributor to the *Pennsylvania Journal* asked if "any State on this continent . . . has treated the Christian religion with so much contempt as our Convention has done?"[23]

The constitution of Delaware (1776) required that all state officers swear a Trinitarian oath. The constitution of South Carolina (1778) actually made "the Christian Protestant religion . . . the established religion of this state." The constitution of Georgia (1777) required that representatives be "of the Protestant religion."[24]

New Jersey's constitution (1776) disqualified non-Protestants implicitly rather than explicitly by stipulating that "all persons, professing a belief in any Protestant sect . . . shall be capable of being elected into any office." A correspondent in the *New Jersey Gazette* singled out this provision for special praise. "The constitution of New Jersey," he wrote, "justly restricts your votes to persons professing a belief in the faith of any protestant sect." Governor William Livingston defended it as a "beautiful" example of religious liberty.[25]

The first constitution proposed for Massachusetts (1778) limited religious freedom to Protestants only, nor could non-Protestants hold state offices. None objected to the latter provision, though it is noteworthy that Berkshire County suggested the constitution be strengthened by an addition stating that "no person ought to be a Member of [the national] Congress unless he is of the Protestant Religion." The second Massachusetts constitution (1780), the work of James Bowdoin, Samuel Adams, and John Adams, was more liberal. All "christians . . . shall be equally under the protection of the law," it specified, and holding office as well was open to Christians. Catholics could qualify by taking a test oath renouncing the superiority of papal authority "in any matter, civil ecclesiastical or spiritual." Sixty-three Massachusetts towns registered objections to the use of the term "Christian" rather than the term "Protestant." Typical were the sentiments of the citizens of Springfield: "As the people of this Commonwealth are generally, if not universally, of the Protestant reformed religion, it would be a matter of Great and General Concern that any Person might ever be elected . . . over them or their Posterity, who should not be of the Protestant Religion."[26]

There were fugitive voices raised against having any religious test oath for office. Joseph Hawley, elected to a seat in the legislature, declined because he regarded such an oath as a contradiction to the inalienable rights of an individual, which other portions of the Massachusetts constitution guaranteed.[27] John Leland, a Baptist preacher, attacked the Massachusetts constitution in 1794 in a pamphlet, *The Yankee Spy*:

> Q. What think you of the Constitution of Massachusetts?
> A. It is as good a performance as could be expected in a state
>   where religious bigotry and enthusiasm have been so
>   predominant.[28]

More in keeping with public opinion was the attitude expressed by Theophilus Parsons some years later. "To enforce the *moral* duties is essential to the welfare of a free state," he noted. "Religion was made a part of the constitution to co-operate with human institutions, and this religion was *Protestant Christianity*."[29]

As in Massachusetts, the demand for political restrictions against non-Protestants in New Hampshire was nearly universal. When William Plumer wrote an essay objecting to the discriminatory clauses in the state constitution (1782), he had to pay the editor of the *New Hampshire Gazette* three dollars to print so radical an opinion. "That system which provides for an equal administration of justice and equality, and preserves the natural rights and privileges of the people in the greatest latitude," Plumer reasoned, "is the best suited to the humor and disposition of freemen. If [the majority] deny that liberty, which they enjoy themselves, to others because their ecclesiastical sentiment is different from theirs, then their determination is partial and unequal. The ideas of power and equality are in their nature distinct, and ought not to be confounded." But Plumer's was a solitary voice.[30]

Connecticut remained without a constitution for more than forty years. The state simply functioned under its original royal charter. Dissenting Protestants were accorded a larger measure of religious liberty in the nineteenth century, although none of Connecticut's various "acts of toleration" afforded political equality for Jews.[31] The same was true of Rhode Island. Contrary to myth, Rhode Island did not grant full religious freedom. Before the American Revolution, Jews lived there "as strangers," not as naturalized citizens. In fact, during 1761–62, the application of two Jews for naturalization was denied.[32] The American Revolution changed nothing. Not until the constitution of 1842 were Rhode Island Jews emancipated politically.

The constitution of New York (1777), was the only one without restrictions on holding office for Jews, who held it up as a model that they wished other states would emulate. The fact that the constitution discriminated against Catholics appeared not to bother Jews one bit.[33] In the constitution of Maryland (1776), the discrimination was precisely the reverse. There one had to declare a belief "in the Christian religion" to hold "any office of trust or profit." Catholics and professing Protestants of any sect possessed full and equal civil rights, while Jews and freethinkers did not.[34] Catholics hoped that Maryland's constitution would become a national model.

No state was wracked by more bitter religious disputes than Virginia. Its constitution (1776) said nothing about religious qualifications for voting and holding office except that practices "shall remain as exercised at present." But in June 1779, when Thomas Jefferson's proposed statute on religious liberty was introduced to the state assem-

bly—with its unequivocal words, "that all men shall be free to profess, and by argument to maintain, their opinions in matters of religion,
and that the same shall in no wise diminish, enlarge, or affect their
civil capacities"—many Virginians regarded it as an attack upon Christianity.[35] Petitions for and against the bill flooded the legislature, and
letters in newspapers argued the wisdom of exalting individual freedom at the expense of majority rights. A contributor to the *Virginia
Gazette* admitted that "Jews, Mohamedans, Atheists or Deists" should
be tolerated, but they had no right to hold public office or to promote
their "singular opinions." A petition from Culpeper County asked the
legislature to reject Jefferson's bill and to substitute one that would in-
stitute a form of Christian religious establishment. After all, the majority of Virginians were Christians. From Amherst County a petition requested that any toleration accorded to Catholics be "guarded and
limited," and that no Catholic, "Jew, Turk, or Infidel," be permitted to
hold any civil or military position in the state.[36]

Public agitation over Jefferson's bill was preempted for a number of
years by other proposals to levy tax assessments to support religion.
George Washington saw nothing wrong with such assessments, especially if the law was not compulsory upon non-Christians. "I am not
amongst the number of those who are so much alarmed at the thought
of making People pay towards the support of that which they profess, if
of the denomination of Christians," he wrote, "or declare themselves
Jews, Mahomitans or otherwise, and thereby obtain proper relief."[37]
But James Madison felt otherwise. He secretly authored and his friend
George Mason actively distributed "A Memorial and Remonstrance"
against the proposed assessment bill. "Who does not see," asked
Madison, "that the same authority which can establish Christianity, in
exclusion of all other Religions, may establish with the same ease any
particular sect of Christians in exclusion of all other Sects? that the
same authority which can force a citizen to contribute three pence only
of his property for the support of any one establishment, may force
him to conform to any other establishment in all cases whatsoever?[38]
Enough Virginians supported Madison's argument, or opposed assessment for other reasons, to assure its defeat.

Madison then reintroduced Jefferson's bill on religious freedom,
which finally passed in 1786, but not before last-minute attempts were
made to alter the wording of the preamble. Madison later recalled that
a proposal "to insert the words 'Jesus Christ' after the words 'our lord'

in the preamble" would have implied "a restriction of the liberty defined in the bill to those professing his religion only."[39] The rejection of
this amendment, Jefferson noted, was "proof" that the legislature
"meant to comprehend, within the mantle of its protection, the Jew
and Gentile, the Christian and Mahometan, the Hindoo, and infidel of
every denomination."[40] With understandable pride, Jefferson wrote to
Madison from France, where he served as American minister:

> The Virginia Act for Religious Freedom has been received
> with infinite approbation in Europe, and propagated with enthu-
> siasm. I do not mean by the governments, but by the individuals
> who compose them. It has been translated into French and Ital-
> ian, has been sent to most of the courts of Europe. . . . It is
> inserted in the new Encyclopedia, and is appearing in most of
> the publications respecting America. . . . It is honorable for us
> to have produced the first legislature who had the courage to
> declare that the reason of man may be trusted with the formation
> of his own opinions.[41]

Federalists and Anti-Federalists

The impact of Jefferson's statute upon the founding fathers cannot be denied. Article 6, section 3, was incorporated into the
federal Constitution with little debate. A few delegates, Luther Martin
of Maryland commented, were "so unfashionable as to think . . . that
in a Christian country, it would be at least decent to hold out some
distinction between the professors of Christianity and downright infidelity or paganism."[42] These few were easily outvoted. The delegates
from North Carolina opposed Article 6, section 3, and those from
Maryland and Connecticut were divided. All the remaining ballots
were affirmative.

During the ratification debates in the various states, Article 6, section 3, proved not to be a significant issue. To be sure, there were a
number of Anti-Federalists—opponents of the Constitution—who
complained of the lack of a religious test for holding office.[43] At the
Massachusetts ratifying convention Major Thomas Lusk, a delegate
from West Stockbridge, "shuddered at the idea that Roman Catholics,
Papists, and Pagans might be introduced into office."[44] At the New

Hampshire convention, Deacon Matthias Stone expressed his alarm that the absence of a religious test "would leave the Bible, that precious jewel, that pearl of great price, without support." He feared "the blood of all the martyrs would rise up against us." Another speaker suggested that at least the president ought to be compelled to take a proper religious oath, otherwise, "a Turk, a Jew, a Roman Catholic, and what is worse than all, a Universalist, may be President of the United States."[45] At the North Carolina convention the Reverend David Caldwell again warned that the lack of a religious test amounted to "an invitation for Jews and pagans of every kind to come among us. At some future period this might endanger the character of the United States."[46] "Curtiopolis," writing in the New York *Daily Advertiser*, noted that the Constitution "gives the command of the whole militia to the President—should he hereafter be a Jew our dear posterity may be ordered to rebuild Jerusalem."[47]

One scholar concludes that the prejudiced views of these Anti-Federalists against non-Protestants "would not have been expressed so vigorously . . . had they not represented a sizable constituent opinion."[48] Yet, with the exception of Luther Martin, not a single important Anti-Federalist writer or orator attacked Article 6, section 3.[49] Their silence can be interpreted as indifference or approval. More important, some Anti-Federalists singled out Article 6, section 3, for special praise. In North Carolina, for example, the leading Anti-Federalist debater, Samuel Spencer, spoke forcefully against religious tests for holding office. Such tests, he remarked, "had been the foundation of persecutions in all countries." He wished "every other part" of the Constitution "was as good and proper."[50] Another Anti-Federalist, a Pennsylvanian using the pseudonym William Penn, pinpointed "the contradictions of the human mind" to be found in the state constitutions, which guaranteed religious freedom "as a part of the natural rights of the citizens" and then expressly denied those rights in "practice."[51] Indeed, the only major Anti-Federalist objection to the Constitution touching upon the subject of religion was its failure to include a written bill of rights.

These facts, combined with the unanimous support of Federalists for Article 6, section 3, make it appear that religious liberty was a nearly universal sentiment of the American public. The Constitution "puts all sects on the same footing," explained Edmund Randolph in its defense. "A man of abilities and character, of any sect whatever, may be admitted to any office or public trust under the United States."[52] Tench Coxe's pamphlet cited the official prejudice of other nations. "In Italy, Spain, and Portugal," Coxe wrote, "no protestant can hold a public trust. In England every Presbyterian, and other persons not of their established church, is incapable of holding an office. No such impious deprivation of the rights of men can take place under the new federal constitution."[53] The Reverend John Leland boasted that "one of the great excellencies of the Constitution is that no religious test is ever to be required to qualify any officer."[54]

But a closer reading of Federalist support for Article 6, section 3, reveals that many did so for tactical rather than for philosophical reasons; that their definition of religious liberty was limited to Christians or to Protestants or even to certain Protestants; and that what they approved on the national level was not acceptable to them in their own states. One must bear in mind a crucial distinction in purpose between Article 6, section 3, and the later Bill of Rights. The former was written to protect government *from* religion; the latter to protect religion *from* government. A primary reason for Article 6, section 3, was to guarantee that no one sect or combination of sects would ever become so powerful—as in England—so as to design a religious test oath that would exclude others from office on the national level. Not all Federalists thought along these lines, but many did so, and they envisioned the American future as a federation of Christian states in which the majority churches would be supported by local compulsory taxation, and the state governments—where real power would reside—would be controlled by Protestants only.

Samuel Livermore, a leading New Hampshire Federalist, offers a case in point. In his classic study *Church and State in the United States*, Anson P. Stokes wrote that "probably no other name . . . of those who have contributed to the cause of religious freedom is so little known to the public as that of Livermore." Stokes devoted many pages to Livermore, lauding him for providing "the original proposal which was made the basis of Congressional debate on religious freedom guarantees." He "was mainly responsible for putting his state squarely on record in favor of religious freedom." As president of the New Hampshire convention of 1791–92, Stokes continued, Livermore was instrumental in the adoption of a state bill of rights that "protected rights of conscience in almost exactly the same form that these were provided for in the constitution of 1784."[55]

But at that 1791 convention, Stokes neglected to mention, William Plumer forced a vote on a proposition to remove all religious qualifications for holding office from the state constitution. Plumer pointed out that a religious test was "incompatible with the principles of a free government, and inconsistent with the bill of rights."[56] Livermore voted against it. So did eight other Federalists who had supported the federal Constitution three years earlier.[57] Nor is there any evidence that these men in future years sought to end the system of religious taxes in New Hampshire. They endorsed Article 6, section 3, as a pragmatic measure. On home grounds they concurred with the reasoning of a contemporary, Jeremy Belknap, that "there is . . . as entire religious liberty in New Hampshire as any people can rationally desire."[58]

Oliver Ellsworth of Connecticut is another example of a Federalist who is often lauded by scholars for his defense of religious liberty.[59] A delegate to the Philadelphia convention, Ellsworth rebutted Anti-Federalist criticisms of the Constitution in a series of letters published in *The Connecticut Courant* in 1787–88. He particularly applauded Article 6, section 3, on the grounds that a religious test in favor of "any one denomination of Christians would be absurd"; that a religious test was of "no security at all," because unprincipled men would take it as a "mere formality"; that "civil government has no business to meddle with the private opinions of people."[60] But Ellsworth's actions surely were contrary to his words, at least as far as his own state was concerned. Connecticut law discriminated not only against Jews, Catholics, and atheists, but also against dissenting Protestants. In 1802 a "Dissenters' Petition"—also called a "Baptist Petition" and an "Infidel Petition"—asked for the elimination of laws favoring the Congregational church, so "as not to interfere with the natural rights of freemen, nor the sacred rights of conscience, in any case whatsoever." Ellsworth, then governor of Connecticut, is alleged to have thrown the petition on the floor, stamped on it, and exclaimed: "This is where it belongs."[61] In time, dissenting Protestants in Connecticut gained a measure of equality. Jews and Catholics had to wait longer.

One of the best statements differentiating between religious toleration and religious liberty was penned by William Livingston. A New Jersey delegate to the Philadelphia convention, and governor of that state for fourteen years, he was largely responsible for New Jersey's quick and unanimous ratification of the Constitution. The laws of England, Livingston once explained, do not prohibit the people of that country from attending the church of their choice. Those laws

> do not peremptorily inhibit a man from worshipping God, according to the dictates of his own conscience; nor positively constrain him to violate it, by conforming to the religion of the state. But they punish him for doing the former; or, what amounts to the same thing, for omitting the latter; and consequently punish him for his religion. For, what are the civil disqualifications, and the privation of certain privileges he thereby incurs, but so many punishments?[62]

In contrast, Livingston described how New Jersey's constitution renounced "all discrimination between men, on account of their sentiments about the various modes of church government, or the different articles of their faith." But the portions of the New Jersey constitution that Livingston cited were those which restricted office to Protestants. In 1788 Mathew Carey, publisher of *The American Museum*, took Livingston to task for his defense of New Jersey's constitution. "Are protestants the only capable or upright men in the state?" asked Carey. "Is not the Roman Catholic hereby disqualified? Why so? Will not every argument in defense of his exclusion, tend to justify the intolerance and persecutions of Europe?"[63] More than half a century passed before the restrictive portions of the New Jersey constitution were rescinded.

There were many Protestants who favored the religious provisions of the federal Constitution but who were equally firm in their determination to resist any changes in their state constitutions. Livingston's more famous father-in-law, John Jay, recognized no inconsistency between his strong endorsement of the federal Constitution and his responsibility for New York's restrictions against Catholics. Isaac Backus approved of both the federal Constitution with no religious test oath and the Massachusetts constitution with its Christian test oath. No one was more aware of the prejudices of the Protestant majority than James Madison. It is somewhat ironic, but Madison, father of the Bill of Rights, initially believed that freedom of religion would best be protected as an assumed natural right rather than by a written law. As early as 1788 he informed Jefferson of his fears "that a positive declaration of some of the most essential rights could not be obtained in the requisite latitude. I am sure that the rights of conscience in particular, if submitted to public definition, would be narrowed much more than they are likely ever to be by an assumed power."[64] A few years later, while engaged in the task of drafting a bill of rights, Madison felt it would be more meaningful if it could be made binding upon the states as well as the federal government. That goal was scarcely possible, given state jealousies and Protestant prejudices, and his proposal to Congress for an amendment that "*no state* shall violate the equal rights of conscience" was not adopted.[65] Other founding fathers admitted that what was wise for the nation was improbable for particular states. John Adams, for example, declared "that a change in the solar system might be expected as soon as a change in the ecclesiastical system of Massachusetts."[66] Not until 1820 did he publicly challenge the religious tests for holding office in his state.

Jews Celebrate the Constitution

By the close of the Revolution, and because of it, American Jews became more aware of their status in society. Previously they had seemed to be content with toleration; now they sought liberty. Previously they had petitioned as individuals for a specific privilege; now they petitioned as a group for equality. One Jewish leader in particular, Gershom Seixas, scanned the new state constitutions with great care, sensitive to the different discriminatory provisions each contained.[67] In 1783 a memorial to the Pennsylvania legislature, signed by Philadelphia Jews "in behalf of themselves and their brethren Jews, residing in Pennsylvania," objected to the "religious test" that "deprives Jews of the most eminent rights of freemen, solemnly ascertained to all men who are not professed Atheists." The memorial referred to their revolutionary services, their economic contributions, their exemplary conduct, and their love of liberty. It also contained a threat. It warned that "the disability of Jews to take [a] seat among the representatives of the people [in Pennsylvania]" might well "determine their free choice to go to New York." It spoke of the contradiction between a religious test for holding office and the express statement in the Pennsylvania declaration of rights that "no man who acknowledges the being of a God can be justly deprived or abridged of any civil rights as a citizen on account of his religious sentiments." The text of the memorial was printed in at least two Philadelphia newspapers, *The Freeman's Journal* and *The Independent Gazette*. The latter editorialized as follows:

> The Jews on this continent have ever demeaned themselves as good and worthy subjects, and have been peculiarly firm and united in the great cause of America; and therefore are, of right, entitled to all the privileges and immunities of her mild and equal government, in common with every other order of people. And it is an absurdity, too glaring and inconsistent to find a single advocate, to say a man, or a society, is Free, without possessing and exercising a right to elect and to be elected.[68]

Whatever the mixed motives of the founding fathers in drafting and supporting Article 6, section 3, American Jews immediately recognized and rejoiced in the Constitution as a liberating document.[69] In Savannah they acknowledged "the benedictions of Heaven" for "the energy of federal influence." They thanked George Washington for helping to create a government that "enfranchised us with all the privileges and immunities of free citizens, and initiated us into the grand mass of legislative mechanism." The Jews of Newport wrote to Washington in a similar vein: "Deprived as we have hitherto been of the invaluable rights of free citizens, we now (with a deep sense of gratitude to the Almighty Disposer of all events), behold a Government . . . which to bigotry gives no sanction, to persecution no assistance— but generously affording to All liberty of conscience, and immunities of citizenship—deeming every one, of whatever nation, tongue, or language equal parts of the great governmental machine." The Jews of Philadelphia, New York, Charleston, and Richmond wrote a joint letter of appreciation to Washington that distinguished between his military and political contributions. "Not to your sword alone is our present happiness to be ascribed; That indeed opened the way to the reign of freedom, but never was it perfectly secure, till your hand gave birth to the federal constitution." Washington answered in kind. "It is now no more that toleration is spoken of," he told the Newport congregation, "as if it was by the indulgence of one class of people, that another enjoyed the exercise of their inherent natural rights." The "spirit of liberality and philanthropy" will certainly spread, he predicted to the

Savannah congregation, "and your brethren will benefit thereby in proportion as it shall become still more extensive." [70]

   The *"spirit of liberality" did spread, but at a much slower pace than George Washington might have thought.* [71] *From the ratification of the Constitution to the post–Civil War period American Jews were aware of attempts to Christianize the federal government. Even as George Washington was being inaugurated, the ministers and ruling elders of the "First Presbytery Eastward, in Massachusetts and New Hampshire," reminded him that "we should not have been alone in rejoicing to have seen some* explicit *acknowledgment of THE TRUE ONLY GOD, AND JESUS CHRIST whom he has sent, inserted somewhere in the Magna Carta of our country."* [72] *In the nineteenth century the attempt to restore Protestant Christianity to a position of political primacy became a major goal as the Enlightenment waned and a resurgence of evangelicalism swept America.*

There Is No God But Liberty, No Gospel But the Constitution

With the ratification of the Constitution and the enactment of a Bill of Rights, it is commonly believed that religious freedom was achieved. According to one scholar, "in a few states the older [discriminatory] provisions lingered, but without the capacity to resist any sustained attack. They were so discordant with the beliefs to which all Americans subscribed, that they disappeared as soon as their invidious character was challenged."[1] The Constitution did set an example for four states, which, between 1789 and 1792, altered their constitutions to correspond to that of Virginia and the federal government. Delaware abandoned its requirement of a Trinitarian oath. Pennsylvania removed its references to the New Testament, permitting Jews to hold office but continuing to bar atheists. South Carolina and Georgia struck all religious restrictions. Nevertheless, eight other states did not, with several refusing to make any changes for many decades.

Each state had a distinct character that resulted from the interaction of its geographic location, cultural inheritance, ethnic composition, economic structure, and dominant religious persuasions. Jews had as much trouble ending constitutional discriminations in Maryland and North Carolina as they did in Massachusetts and New Hampshire. Bigotry crossed party lines and locations. Indeed, bigotry

> *prevailed over party in numerous instances. Yet in*
> *the North, with good reason, most Jews perceived*
> *Federalists to be their enemies, which was not the*
> *case in the South.*

Jews and Political Parties

With the rise of political parties in the 1790s, a number of Jews began to participate actively in politics. One would assume
that most would favor the Federalists, because that party identified itself with the Constitution, which Jews immediately recognized granted
them an equality that the states did not. Moreover, Jews revered the
figure of George Washington, who, with each passing year, was viewed
more as a Federalist partisan. The same kind of biting anti-Semitic references made by a number of Anti-Federalists in their opposition to the
ratification of the Constitution were repeated by Republicans who opposed Alexander Hamilton's financial program in the 1790s. One such
writer condemned speculators for their "Israeltish avarice." Another
charged that Hamilton's policies were enriching "British riders, Am-
sterdam Jews, American Tories, and speculating lawyers and doctors."[2] A poet put his grievances to verse:

> A public debt's a public blessing,
> Which 'tis of course a crime to lessen.
> Every day a fresh report he [Hamilton] broaches,
> That spies and Jews may ride in coaches,
> Soldier and farmer don't dispair,
> Untax'd as yet are earth and air.[3]

Indeed, a number of Jews did become Federalists and remained stal-
wartly so, but they were a distinct minority. There was good reason
that the majority favored the Republicans. First of all, despite obvious
exceptions to the contrary, members of the Federalist party, especially
in the northern states, were the chief opponents of religious liberty for
non-Christians. Initially, as we have noted, they sought to preserve the
privileged status of their churches from the pressures of dissenting
Protestant denominations (generally Republican); when that was no
longer possible they sought, at a minimum, to have the law recognize

the superior rights of Christian to non-Christian citizens. On the national level they accepted the religious equality clauses of the Constitution as a wise and necessary compromise; on the state level, in time, while they were forced by circumstances to concede equality to Baptists and Unitarians and Catholics, they saw no reason to extend it to Jews and Mohammedans and atheists. John Adams could claim to have "read himself out of bigotry," though his remarks about particular religious groups lead one to believe otherwise. Adams did oppose religious qualifications for holding office, yet he consistently endorsed a system of tax-supported churches in Massachusetts. His son, John Quincy Adams—whom one scholar calls "the last of the Enlightened presidents"—rarely missed an opportunity to speak of Jews in a disparaging way: "the alien Jew," "the squeaking of the Jew delegate," "Jew-brokering tricks," et cetera.[4] Other Federalists were not so liberal as either of the Adamses.

As a group, Federalists identified government with morality, and many went one step further, identifying morality with Christianity. Unless citizens were Christian, they could not be moral. Unless they were moral, republicanism could not survive. That a number of Jews equated Federalists with Christian bigotry early on could be read in the passionate response of Benjamin Nones to the crude anti-Semitic jibe in the Philadelphia press in 1800, which mocked his religion, his poverty, and his Republican sympathies. "I am a Jew," wrote Nones, "and if for no other reason, for that reason I am a republican." Nones hit at "the pious priesthood of church establishments" by whom Jews "are compassionately ranked with Turks, Infidels, and Heretics."[5] Jews "have *not* sacrificed our principles to our interest" nor abandoned "our religious duties." As for morality, Nones charged, it was those who derided Jews for their faith who lacked "principles, moral or religious, to guide their conduct."[6]

When an English novel, *The Democrat*, was reprinted in New York, a Federalist editor wrote a separate preface identifying American subversives (the Democratic Society) as an "itinerant gang" who "will easily be known by their physiognomy; they all seem to be, like their Vice President [Solomon Simpson, a Jewish merchant], of the tribe of Shylock, they have that leering underlook, and malicious grin, that seem to say to the honest man—*approach me* not." Even non-Jews with Jewish names experienced Federalist anti-Semitism. Thus, when Benjamin Rush, a Republican, sued William Cobbett, a Federalist, for libel and won, Cobbett blamed the "diabolical" legal argument of one of Rush's attorneys, Moses Levy. Such an argument, Cobbett claimed, "never could have been engendered but in the mind of a Jew!" But it was understandable: "I cannot . . . muster up anything like anger against a poor devil like Moses; he did not believe a word that he said; he vash vorking for de monish, dat vash all." Levy was an Episcopalian. Moreover, Cobbett was well aware of that fact, but it served his purpose to portray him as a Jew. Similarly, when John Israel started a Jeffersonian newspaper called *Tree of Liberty* in Pittsburgh in 1800, Federalists denounced his "Jew press" for its "Jacobinism" and "sedition." Israel was not Jewish. Nor was the man Charles Nisbet, a Federalist, described to a friend as "a Jewish Tavern Keeper, with a very Jewish name," who "is chosen one of the Senators of this commonwealth for the city of Philadelphia solely on account of his violent attachment to the French Interests."[7]

Nevertheless, Federalists tried to attract Jewish votes in 1800—insignificant as their number was—by labeling Jefferson an atheist. A letter signed "Moses S. Solomons" appeared first in the *Philadelphia Gazette*, then in New York, describing the author as "a follower of Moses and the Old Testament" and inviting his coreligionists in the "COMMON CAUSE" of defeating Thomas Jefferson, who denied the existence of God and who opposed "all religion." There followed a letter signed by "A Christian" congratulating Solomons, concluding that his testimony "is the more valuable because he is a Jew." Benjamin Nones soon denounced the Solomons letter as a spurious document, and the Philadelphia synagogue issued a statement published in the *Aurora* that "no such man as Moses S. Solomons has *ever been*, or is now a member of the Hebrew congregation of this city," adding that the purpose of the ruse was "intended, no doubt," for "political ends."[8]

The Solomons letter and its exposure as a fraud probably served to confirm Jewish assumptions of Federalist anti-Semitism. Certainly there was sufficient evidence of it among many of the Federalist elite. Jefferson and Jews were equally anathema to them. Typical were the forebodings of the Federalist Joseph Dennie of New Hampshire, an aspiring writer who served briefly as Secretary of State Timothy Pickering's personal secretary and who threatened to leave the United States if Jefferson came to power. "It will then be time for a man of my feelings and principles to abandon public life, and, perhaps, even my country," he wrote his parents from Philadelphia. For "this region" was "covered" with a "Jewish and canting and cheating" public with no respect for traditional political and cultural institutions. (He did not leave.)[9]

Especially after Thomas Jefferson became president in 1801, Federalists turned their cause into a Christian crusade against the forces of infidelity represented by the Republicans.[10] Alexander Hamilton cynically but seriously proposed the formation of a Christian Constitutional Society. Citizens joining the organization would unite under the twin banners of its title, but its true purpose was to guide them back to political sanity and thus to restore the fortunes of the Federalist party. Surprisingly, a few even attacked the Constitution itself as a godless document. The Reverend John M. Mason, a well-known New York Federalist, complained that "from the Constitution of the United States it is impossible to ascertain what God we worship, or whether we own a God at all."[11] An anonymous Federalist writer in the *Farmer's Weekly Museum* criticized the founding fathers: "These *great men*, who had *acted in secret*, began to declare themselves openly—'There is no God but liberty; no gospel but the Constitution.' "[12]

The return of Thomas Paine to America in 1802, with his travel in a public vessel having been authorized by Thomas Jefferson, triggered a furious Federalist attack. The *United States Gazette* editorialized, "Shall we suffer a professed Deist to take his residence among us? Christianity is a subject that is too sublime for investigation, too sacred for discussion." The *Green Mountain Patriot* predicted, "Let all remaining regard for the principles of Christianity be obliterated from the minds of your fellow citizens, and this land would soon be a field of blood." One Republican, calling himself a "Friend to Religion and Order," responded that these "alarms, that the foundation of the Christian religion were undermined, were greatly increased by the representations of our Anglo-Federalists." Another Republican declared that the "clergy of the day have enlisted themselves under the banner of a malignant party . . . The Tory Federalists."[13]

"*Religion and Morality*," Timothy Pickering toasted at a Washington birthday celebration in 1804, "essential supports of a *free government*."[14] By religion he meant Christianity, and Federalists in defeat seemed more determined than ever that their faith had to be defended and encouraged by every means, and by positive legislation and legal recognition as the law of the land. Some decades later, Daniel Webster, in the Federalist tradition, argued before the Supreme Court that "charity" stemmed solely from Christianity, therefore Stephen Girard's will to establish a training school that forbade any religious teaching was not a charity. No other religion but Christianity would do, said Webster. "When little children were brought into the presence of the Son of God, his disciples proposed to send them away; but he said, 'Suffer little children to come unto me.' Unto *me*; he did not send them first for lessons in morals to the schools of the Pharisees or to the unbelieving Sadducees, nor to read the precepts and lessons *phylacteried* on the garments of the Jewish priesthood." [15]

Connecticut, Massachusetts, New York, and New Hampshire

Connecticut, four decades after the American Revolution, (1818), disestablished the Congregational church. "The exercise and enjoyment of religious profession and worship, without discrimination," the new state constitution stated, "shall forever be free to all persons in this state." Thomas Jefferson expressed his delight to John Adams "that this den of the priesthood is at length broken up, and that a protestant popedom is no longer to disgrace the American history and character." [16] Jews could now hold office. In other respects, however, Jews were *not* legally equal. The Connecticut constitution provided not for the equality of "powers, rights, and privileges" of all religions, but only of "every society or denomination of Christians in this state." The wording was carefully chosen after a long and earnest debate on the matter by delegates. The clear alternative of recognizing the equality of *every* religion by omitting the word "Christian" was rejected by the convention. [17] One member who favored keeping the word "Christian" explained that there was no prejudice in his vote. He was "willing to tolerate Jews and Mohammedans," but "there had never been any in the State and probably never would be." [18] Actually, the first record of a Jew living in Connecticut was dated as early as 1659. The total number long remained minuscule, and how many Jews were resident in Connecticut in 1818 is unknown. [19] The fact remains that in the decision of the convention there was more than a "hint," as one scholar has concluded, "of discrimination against the Hebrew and possibly the Unitarian." [20]

In effect the Connecticut constitution recognized Christianity as the religion of the state. Yet so conservative was the population, and still so powerful were the Congregationalists, that the constitution was barely ratified, 13,918 to 12,354. Non-Congregational Protestants, united as the "Toleration party," celebrated their victory, for they gained immediate equality. Jews had to wait a few decades more. By the 1840s Connecticut exhibited further signs of an expanding liberalism. The mayor of New Haven, together with Yale College, invited a New York rabbi to lecture on "The Present Condition and Future Spiritual and Temporal Hopes of the Jews." The number of Jews increased sufficiently to form a congregation, and in 1843 a special enactment of the state legislature provided "that Jews who may desire to unite and form religious societies, shall have the same rights, powers and privileges which are given to Christians."[21]

The degree of resistance to granting non-Protestants or non-Christians political equality could also be measured in Massachusetts, which adopted a new constitution in 1821. As in Connecticut, the proposal to remove the religious test for holding office succeeded, but it was not easily accomplished. At the state convention Daniel Webster supported the proposal with a speech so lukewarm and so laden with reservations, that it could have been—and was—used by the opposition. Webster first established the right of the majority to set constitutional qualifications for holding office on the basis of religion, as they could for age, property, or residence. Then he conceded that he was quite willing "to retain" the religious oath. "If others were satisfied with it, I should be." He endorsed its removal purely on the grounds of expediency; that is, it was not "essential" since "there is another part of the constitution which recognizes in the fullest manner the benefits which civil society derives from those Christian institutions which cherish piety, morality and religion. I am conscious that we should not strike out of the constitution all recognition of the Christian religion."[22]

Leverett Saltonstall, like Webster a Federalist, predicted the ruin of Massachusetts if the religious test was removed. "As to jews, mahometans, deists, and atheists," Saltonstall thundered, "they are all opposed to the common religion of the Commonwealth and believe it an imposition, a mere fable, and that its professors are under a wretched delusion. Are such persons suitable rulers of a Christian state?" Jacob Tuckerman, a Unitarian minister, agreed. "Either the religion of Jesus Christ is from God or it is not. Either we are accountable to God for all our means and opportunities of advancing the interests of this religion, or we are not," he stated. "If men should be elevated to high and responsible stations, who are enemies of Christianity, may we not look with some apprehension to the consequences?" Samuel Hubbard, as did Webster, denied that holding office was "an inalienable right." He saw no reason to alter the 1780 constitution in this regard: "We were a Christian people then; and are we not now? And do not the same reasons continue for supporting the Christian religion?" [23]

Of those who spoke to remove the religious test, James Prince reminded the convention that although there were only two "*positive* instances" of elected officers who could not or would not take the oath since 1780, "there may have been many *negative* ones" who were precluded because of it. (Prince was referring to Joseph Hawley, a devout Christian, who refused to accept a legislative seat because of his belief that civil government had no right to compel anyone to make a profession of their faith; and Ebenezer Seaver of Roxbury, who declined because he did not accept Christianity and therefore could not subscribe to the test oath. "It is singular," William Plumer noted, "that the same test should exclude both the conscientious *believer* and the honest *unbeliever*.") Henry Dearborn insisted that the test "was an unjust exaction and a violation of the unalienable rights of the people." James T. Austin, a Republican attorney from Boston, directly challenged Webster's logic. Age, property, and residence are proper qualifications a state can demand, Austin reasoned, "because they are necessary to insure the proper performance of the duties of office." Religion is not. "This was the distinction," he stated, and "if we pass this line there is no place to stop." Besides, "the Christian religion needs not oaths or tests to protect it any more than it does force." [24]

The people of Massachusetts voted to drop the religious test for office, 13,782 to 12,480. However, without Suffolk County (Boston), which approved the change by a substantial margin of 2,464 to 211, it would have failed. [25] Still another dozen years passed before other Christian references in the Massachusetts constitution were struck in 1833 so that, finally, all religious sects and denominations were equally under the protection of the law.

The right to hold office was not an issue in New York. Jews possessed that right in the initial constitution of 1777. Catholics gained it when the state legislature in 1806 changed the law to permit Francis Cooper, a Republican of that faith, to take a revised oath and to occupy a seat in the assembly. Some members of the "federal party," a Catholic priest informed Bishop John Carroll, "indulged their illiberality so far as to cast upon us all the filthy dregs of prejudice and animosity,"[26] but to no avail. The bill revising the oath passed the assembly sixty-three to twenty-six, and the senate with only one dissenting vote. Yet when New York held a constitutional convention in 1821, the perennial problem of religion and government was once more debated—and with considerable venom.

Some years earlier a man named Ruggles had been arrested, tried, and convicted for blasphemy. He had said in public that "Jesus Christ was a bastard, and his mother must be a whore." (He was sentenced to three months in jail and fined $500.) Despite the fact that Ruggles had broken no written law—there was no statute defining blasphemy—and that he had not endangered public safety, the state supreme court upheld the conviction. Chancellor James Kent ruled that it was legal to blaspheme any non-Christian religion, "and for this plain reason, that the case assumed we are a christian people, and the morality of the country is deeply grafted upon christianity, and not upon the doctrines or worship of those imposters." To blaspheme Christianity, on the other hand, was to violate the common law.[27]

That logic was unacceptable to some Republicans at the New York convention. (After all, Thomas Jefferson had composed an argument that asserted the contrary.) General Erastus Root, a freethinking Republican, moved to add a section to the constitution depriving the judiciary of the power to "declare any particular religion to be the law of the land" or to "exclude any witness on account of his religious faith." Root argued that Jews held state office. Indeed, a Jew currently served as sheriff of a large city. By the implication of the Ruggles decision "he is guilty of blasphemy every time he enters a synagogue," for that could be considered an anti-Christian act. Kent, a member of the convention, responded that the authors of the 1777 constitution "meant to preserve . . . the morals of the country, which rested on christianity as the foundation. They meant to apply the principles of common law against blasphemy, which they did not believe the constitution ever meant to abolish. Are we not a christian people? Do not ninety-nine hundredths of our fellow citizens hold the general truths of the Bible to be dear and sacred?"[28]

Root divided his motion in two parts, and the convention defeated both. That "no witness shall ever be questioned as to his religious faith" was rejected, ninety-four to eight; that "no particular religion shall ever be declared or adjudged to be the law of the land" lost by a vote of seventy-four to forty-one. The old Federalist stalwart, Rufus King, reflected the view of the majority in stating that "while all mankind are by our constitution tolerated . . . yet the religious professions of the Pagan, the Mahometan, and the Christian, are not, in the eye of the law, of equal truth and excellence." [29]

New Hampshire usually followed the example of Massachusetts, but in the matter of non-Protestant political rights the people of the Granite State proved as obdurate as their native stone. Under Federalist control the idea of religious liberty scarcely penetrated; later on, ironically, as the most Democratic of northern states, New Hampshire earned the dubious distinction of being the last to remove its religious qualification for holding office.

An indication of just how seriously New Hampshire citizens took their religion can be gleaned from a 1791 debate over a blasphemy bill. One legislator, who wanted to empower magistrates "with authority to avenge *insults on God*," proposed that anyone "convicted of *speaking disrespectfully of any part of the bible should have their tongues bored thro with a hot iron*." William Plumer, who recorded the episode, was appalled, especially at the tongue-in-cheek suggestion of another speaker, John Sherburne, a man noted for his "hypocrisy and contempt of religion." Sherburne seconded the amendment but claimed it really did not go far enough: Convicted blasphemers should be put to death. Plumer feared that the legislators would react in anger to Sherburne's ridicule.

> I was apprehensive if that amendment passed, fanatical bigots, urged by unprincipled political partisans, when the public mind was seized with frenzy, might prosecute and injure men more virtuous than themselves. I was aware of the strong prejudices of some of the members against me on account of my religious tenets, and doubted whether my opposition, instead of defeating, would not insure its adoption. But perceiving from the temper of the house, and the conduct of such men as Sherburne, that there was danger of its passing, I could not remain silent. I rose, and tho deeply affected and strongly agitated, I made one of the best

speeches as I think I ever made on any subject. I endeavored to demonstrate that the amendment was hostile to the principles and temper not only of christianity but of sound policy, and pregnant with danger. I made more than twenty appropriate quotations from the bible—contrasted the arbitrary and oppressive system of judaism with the mildness and benevolence of christianity—and closed with a strong appeal to the better and more liberal feelings of the human heart. The motion was rejected, *tho not by a large majority.*[30]

Plumer served as governor in the nineteenth century. He confided to his diary in 1818 that "there is no such thing as absolute religious freedom," having struggled in vain to achieve that goal for three decades. "It is true a man may think as he pleases, but he cannot communicate his thoughts to the public, if he differs from them, without rendering himself obnoxious to the people.[31] Some progress was achieved, but not for Catholics and Jews. The religious issues that predominated in the political struggles between Federalists and Republicans were wholly within the Protestant community. Republican victory led to the passage of a Toleration Act in 1819, which was condemned by Federalist-Congregationalists as a "repeal of the Christian religion," which they felt was tantamount to "abolishing the Bible."[32] The act, in fact, neither separated church and state nor helped non-Protestants. The state courts made it plain that New Hampshire was a "Christian state," which clearly meant "Protestant," although they were forced to wrestle with definitions of those words in numerous suits between Unitarians and Trinitarians.

Joining William Plumer in the cause of religious liberty was Isaac Hill (who also served as governor), publisher of *The New Hampshire Patriot.* That paper defended the delivery of mail on Sunday, because to do otherwise was to violate the separation of church and state; supported Abner Kneeland, who was tried and convicted of blasphemy in Massachusetts; and frequently argued in behalf of Catholics, Jews, Shakers, Universalists, and other minority groups. Even the state of Alabama secured "to every [white] person that his religion shall not be a bar to his holding an office," Hill editorialized, but "our Constitution, to our discredit, does contain a religious test. . . . Does any one pretend, in this enlightened day, that a pious and conscientious Catholic is less worthy to be a governor than many persons who call themselves protestants?" (In the first decades of the nineteenth century there was only a handful of Catholics in New Hampshire and no documentation of any permanent Jewish residents.)[33]

Why did a majority of New Hampshire citizens, a state controlled by the Democratic party during and after the age of Jackson (the Congregationalist minority remaining Whig, as they had been Federalist) reject the pleas of their political leaders to change the constitution? Part of the reason had to do with timing. A constitutional convention, not a legislative act, was necessary to accomplish the change, and no convention was held for nearly six decades. And during this period anti-Catholicism, at a low ebb during the age of Jefferson, mounted steadily. As early as 1834 New Hampshire nativists forcefully drove Irish Catholic workers from the town of Concord. By the time a constitutional convention was held in 1850, nativism was at its peak and cut across party lines. The xenophobia of New Hampshire citizens not only increased but became calcified. At the 1850 convention Judge Levi Woodbury remarked, "In the bill of rights you pledge to all sects equality, but afterwards by this [religious] test you make all but protestants unequal. You promise entire freedom of conscience to all and treat it as so high a privilege as not to be in any way inalienable, and yet you leave other than protestants defenseless by disfranchising them from filling offices." The chairman of the convention, Governor Franklin Pierce, supported Woodbury against those delegates who repeated the old allegations that Catholics were antirepublican papists who would, if they could, reinstitute the inquisition. The increased number of Catholics in New Hampshire, nativists insisted, made it all the more necessary to retain the constitutional prohibition. Woodbury's view triumphed at the convention, but the proposed revision striking the words "shall be of the Protestant religion" from the constitution was defeated handily by the voters, 9,566 to 12,082.[34]

A quarter of a century later New Hampshire finally removed its religious qualification for holding office. But it did so by only the slimmest of margins and by concurrently reaffirming its constitutional heritage of Protestantism. Delegates to the state convention of 1876 recommended that the religious test be removed, and the people accepted the change, 28,477 to 14,231. (Because a majority of two-thirds was necessary, the amendment actually passed by only five votes!) However, another part of the New Hampshire constitution, Article 6 of the bill of rights, provided for the local "support and maintenance of public Protestant teachers of piety, religion and morality" and guaranteed the equal protection of the law for "every denomination of christians demeaning themselves quietly." The delegates wrestled with both clauses, repeating arguments that had been used a hundred years earlier. Jonathan Sargent of Concord wanted no change: "The framers of our Constitution were at least considered Protestants, and we, perhaps, ought to say a word in favor of Protestantism in preference to any other religion." William Mason of Moultonborough warned that "if you take the word 'Protestant' out of this article, and sent it to the people of New Hampshire, we all know how many there are who are rather sensitive on this point, and they will reject it at once." Edward Sanborn of Franklin felt that the words did no one any harm: "We have lived under it all our lives; we shall always live in perfect liberty in New Hampshire, and so will every man, be he Greek, Jew, or Gentile." Other delegates wished to strike the clauses as relics of the bigoted past. William C. Sturoc of Sunapee attempted what he considered a reasonable compromise by proposing to remove the entire paragraph containing the clause about "public Protestant teachers" but keeping the following one that referred to "every denomination of christians." John Walker of Claremont objected: "There may be some Jews, and I suppose they ought to stand on an equality before the law." So did Samuel Wheeler of Dover, who once again pointed out "that that word alone—'Christian'—is entirely inconsistent with the further clauses in the Constitution." [35]

The people of New Hampshire were given an opportunity to decide on a halfway measure that removed the single word "Protestant" but kept the "Christian" reference. There were 27,664 votes in favor of this, and 15,903 opposed, which was more than a thousand votes short of the two-thirds majority that was required. In 1889 another constitutional convention recommended the bill of rights be made nonsectarian, and the people rejected the proposal by an even larger margin of 27,737 in favor to 20,048 opposed. The next convention, in 1902, heard a delegate ask if New Hampshire "shall take a backward step to allow the Jews or the pagans or the Mohammedans who come into this country, and who enjoy all the privileges of our institutions, to force us to renounce the great principle which has always been recognized in this country—the principle that this nation and state is rightly grounded on Christian principles." The convention submitted a complicated amendment that in effect changed the word "Protestant" to "Christian" in the first paragraph, and "every denomination of christians" to "all religious sects" in the second. The people promptly rejected it, 16,611 in favor to 15,727 opposed. The convention of 1912 repeated the same issues as that of 1902, as well as the result: 16,555 voters who were in favor to 14,315 who were opposed. In 1918 the convention submitted and the people—including women this time—again rejected an attempt to remove the word "Protestant."[36]

The issue was never considered at the convention of 1930, nor at the convention of 1939. It was raised at the convention of 1948, because Eugene Daniel of Franklin introduced a resolution that Article 6 be struck. The resolution was assigned to a Committee on the Bill of Rights, which, apparently, decided that it was better to leave it unreported. Finally, in 1964, a constitutional convention recommended the article's deletion and the substitution of a nonsectarian provision, which was approved in 1968 by a vote of 142,112 to 67,697.[37]

The Maryland "Jew Bill"

In point of time, Jews had to wait nearly as long to achieve political equality in Maryland and North Carolina as they did in Massachusetts and New Hampshire. The reason is twofold. Federalists in the South, a decreasing remnant after 1801, were in many ways a separate breed from their northern brethren. Their historic roots, religious affiliations and economic perspectives were different. To be sure, many equated morality with Christianity, and they joined northern Federalists in picturing Thomas Jefferson as anti-Christian and condemning him for welcoming Thomas Paine, that "domesticated atheist,"[38] back to America. Still, southern Federalists did not need to defend a particular church establishment, viewing it as a bastion against hordes of dissenters, as did the Federalist-Congregationalists in the North. One finds more examples of Federalists willing to speak out for religious liberty in the South than in the North. Such being the case, one finds more examples of Jews (and Catholics) adhering to the Federalist party in the South than in the North. "Learn to know what answer you would return to the Philosophic Unbeliever," ran the advertisement for a Jewish book published by Marcus Levy in Richmond, Virginia, in 1804. The work actually was an old attack upon Voltaire, written by a Jamaican rabbi, but it served, according to the preface, as "a complete answer to those chimerical Philosophers who have adopted that nature imposes upon each individual every necessary restraint, and who with rapid strides are travelling on with man to the perfectability of human nature, as they suppose, but which will be found in the end, to be highly calculated to undermine all rational liberty."[39] For many devout Jews in the South a liberal Federalist was preferable to an infidel Republican. A belief in deism constituted an attack upon Jews as well as upon Christians. Besides, southern Republicans tended to be less liberal than their northern partisans. In the North, Republican strength derived largely from religious dissenters fighting for equality. In the South these dissenters *were* the majority. Simply put, southern Republicans in Maryland and North Carolina split on the issue of extending equality to Jews. Some followed the precepts of their national leaders, Jefferson and Madison; but many others, out of prejudice or fear of antagonizing their rural constituents (in western Maryland, as in western Massachusetts, the bigotry of the farmer prevailed) voted to maintain Christian political purity.

Solomon Etting, a merchant residing in Baltimore and a politically active Republican, first petitioned in 1797 to the Maryland legislature, requesting that it remove the discriminatory constitutional provisions that deprived Jews "of many of the invaluable rights of citizenship." For the next five years, during the quasi war with France, the political turmoil involving the Alien and Sedition Acts, the election of 1800, and the introduction of a new administration, nothing was done. The anomaly of a federal constitution that recognized no religious distinctions, and a state constitution that did, was immediately apparent to Marylanders when Thomas Jefferson appointed Solomon Etting's brother Reuben to the position of United States marshal for Maryland. Under state law no Jew could serve in any office of that sovereignty, even the lowest, or be commissioned in the state militia, or follow the profession of law (because lawyers were considered to be officers of the state as well). Continued petitions from the small Jewish population of Maryland were submitted to the state legislature. With Republicans in power, both nationally and within the state, the "Jew bill" finally was brought to a vote in 1802. It was defeated, thirty-eight to seventeen. Two years later, through the efforts of a nationally prominent Federalist, William Pinkney, it was reintroduced. Pinkney was a moderate Federalist, much respected by Jefferson, who was selected to accompany Monroe on a bipartisan diplomatic mission to England in

1806; later he was chosen as Republican party chief in Baltimore. But Pinkney had little influence outside that city. The fact is that a majority of rural Federalists and rural Republicans felt the same way about the "Jew bill." It was again defeated, thirty-nine to twenty-four.[40]

The idea of a "Jew bill" remained dormant for more than a dozen years. In 1816, "a bill relating to an equality of rights intended for the present purposes was reported in the Senate of Maryland," Jacob I. Cohen reminded Ebenezer S. Thomas, but "was not acted upon, I do not know why." Cohen wanted Thomas to lend his support to a new bill, proposed in 1818 by Thomas Kennedy, a freshman delegate from Washington County. A rather remarkable man, Kennedy was a Presbyterian who recognized and cast off the religious bigotry of his own family and became the steadfast advocate of equality for Jews. The area he represented, in the western part of the state, contained no Jews. Moreover, there were very few in Maryland; but, as Kennedy stated, "if there was only one—to that one, we ought to do justice." Kennedy had long admired Jefferson's contributions to liberty. An amateur poet, he had written verses celebrating the act to establish religious liberty in Virginia. He spoke with passion before the Maryland legislature:

> There is only one opponent that I fear at this time, and that is PREJUDICE—our prejudices, Mr. Speaker, are dear to us, we all know and feel the force of our political prejudices, but our religious prejudices are still more strong, still more dear; they cling to us through life, and scarcely leave us on the bed of death, and it is not the prejudice of a generation, of an age or of a century, that we have now to encounter. No, it is the prejudice which has passed from father to son, for almost eighteen hundred years.[41]

The "narrow, persecuting spirit," Kennedy stated, "is not the spirit of Christianity, and Christianity has suffered much from the officious and misguided zeal of some who call themselves its friends." In a letter to an associate, Kennedy repeated his fear that "Prejudice, Prejudice is against the Bill, and you know prejudice has many votaries." Actually, Kennedy preferred a bill that would eradicate, once and for all, any religious test, not merely one for the relief of Jews. "I must candidly declare that were it left to me, I would abolish the religious test entirely without any exception, and am ready should it meet with the approbation of the House, to submit a motion to that effect, so as to make the bill general." But Kennedy knew that it would be difficult enough to enact a "Jew bill," let alone one that would grant equality to non-believers. Besides, the Jews of Maryland wanted a particular bill for their own emancipation. They were not and did not want to be linked with infidels and atheists.[42]

Kennedy was little known, even in Maryland; but another sponsor of the "Jew bill," Judge Henry M. Brackenridge, enjoyed a moderate international reputation. A lawyer, author, and diplomat, his writings— especially those on South America—were widely published. The speech that he delivered in behalf of equality for Jews therefore received considerable attention and was even translated into German and printed in Berlin. Though a Jeffersonian, Brackenridge argued for the supremacy of a federal Constitution. "I do not hesitate to assert, that could this question be brought before some tribunal competent to decide . . . the right which this bill professes to give is already secured by our national compact. I would boldly contend that the state of Maryland has deprived, and still continues to deprive, American citizens of their just political rights." But no such case was pending; and had there been one, it is doubtful whether any court would have agreed with Brackenridge. (His position, of course, was sustained decades later by judicial interpretations of the Fourteenth Amendment.) Brackenridge disagreed with Kennedy about political rights for non-believers. "I should be the last to deny," he stated, "that a belief in a future state of rewards and punishments is the sheet anchor of all civil government." Jews had such a belief, however, Brackenridge noted, and there was nothing in their religion that would disqualify them from holding office.[43]

On 20 January 1819, the "Jew bill" was defeated, fifty to twenty-four. At the very next session it was again voted upon, and again defeated, forty-seven to twenty. A breakdown of these votes by party shows the Federalists overwhelmingly in opposition, thirty-three to two and nineteen to four against the bill; and the Republicans split, first voting twenty-two to seventeen in its favor, and then twenty-eight to sixteen in opposition. A Tammany newspaper in New York City, the *National Advocate*, edited by Mordecai M. Noah, reported that the loss of the "Jew bill" was due to the hostility of Maryland Catholics, a charge that was quickly denied. Dr. Joshua I. Cohen of Baltimore wrote to Noah explaining that Catholics "within the circle of my acquaintance in this city" had made "liberal expressions" of support. In the Catholic press "not a syllable against the bill" was voiced. Moreover, one Catholic in the upper house, Roger Taney, though a Federalist, spoke forcefully in favor of "abolishing test oaths universally," which was contrary to the views of his fellow party members. Maryland Jews were against such attempts, which were made "contrary to our express wish." Cohen concluded that the prospects for enactment of the "Jew bill" were "brighter than ever before."[44]

Thomas Kennedy, in a poem entitled "To the Children of Israel in Baltimore," also promised better days:

> Your sufferings and your persecution tends
> To increase the zeal and number of your friends,
> They will increase until your feeble foes,
> Your claims to justice shall no more oppose.[45]

Still, five more years elapsed before the bill's final enactment. During this time it was debated at every session, much to the annoyance of a few legislators who objected to the inordinate attention given to what they regarded as an unimportant subject; it became a crucial issue hotly argued in local elections; and it received widespread attention in newspapers all across the country. The dedication of a synagogue in Philadelphia, for example, attended by the chief justice of the state and important Protestant divines, was an instructive lesson, a Pennsylvania reporter commented, as "there are states at no great distance from us to whom it may be useful to behold in this commonwealth, members of the Jewish persuasion are eligible to all public offices, and possess every political right with Christians; that some of our most estimable citizens profess that creed; and withal, that the Christian faith is at least as warmly cherished and as assiduously cultivated here as in any other part of the world." The 1822 Maryland legislature passed the "Jew bill" forty to thirty-three. As a proposed constitutional change, however, it required a majority vote by two consecutive sessions, and the 1823 legislature defeated it, forty-four to twenty-eight. Not until the 1824 and 1825 sessions, by votes of twenty-six to twenty-five and forty-five to thirty-two respectively, did it pass and become the law of the state on 5 January 1826.[46]

Kennedy had nothing to gain politically by championing the cause of the Jews. Quite the opposite, he was subjected to a barrage of invective, labeled "an enemy of Christianity," "Judas Iscariot," and "one half Jew and the other half not a Christian." The bill itself was called "Kennedy's Jew Baby," and in Washington County his campaign was referred to by the opposition as the "Jew ticket." Leading the "Christian ticket" was Benjamin Galloway, a respected and dedicated Republican. In 1823 Galloway warned voters that Kennedy's view threatened society, that his espousal of the "Jew bill" was "an attempt to undervalue and, by so doing, to bring into popular contempt, the Christian religion." Galloway told the people of Washington County that he preferred "Christianity to Judaism, Deism, Unitarianism, or any other new fangled ism." Kennedy was defeated in that election; but a year later he ran again, and this time his dogged persistence; the support he received from other legislators; the pressures of national publicity; and perhaps the logic of his position, which caused voters to rethink theirs, brought him victory.[47]

Much the same reasons applied to explain the change of heart within the Maryland legislature. One of the supporters of the bill, Colonel W. G. D. Worthington, submitted five questions about the number, position, and wealth of Jews in America to Solomon Etting, the Baltimore merchant who nearly three decades before had first petitioned for Jewish equality. Worthington read Etting's responses to the legislature and enlarged upon them to illustrate why the bill should pass: There were some 150 Jews in the state and some 6,000 in the United States, possessing, respectively, by rough estimate, half a million and six million dollars in wealth, thus making a vital economic contribution. Jews had served in both the American Revolution and the War of 1812, they currently occupied high federal positions as diplomats and military officers, and none could doubt their patriotic contribution. To make explicit the injustice of the religious test, Etting recounted a particular incident:

> Early in the spring of the existing year, 1823, a number of spirited young men formed a volunteer corps of riflemen, known by the name of the "Marion Corps"; without any previous knowledge on his part, or even of the existence of this company, they unanimously determined, and did elect Benjamin I. Cohen their captain—a commission was received from Governor Stevens, but not qualified to, of course, in consequence of the existence of the test law. . . . At a meeting of the corps, called for the purpose, it was unanimously determined that no captain should

be elected until the fate of the bill at present before the legislature should be decided, and the corps is, at this time, commanded by the first lieutenant.[48]

After the bill passed, two Jews, Solomon Etting and Jacob I. Cohen, were elected to the Baltimore City Council. Both took the oath that the new law prescribed for state officers professing "the Jewish Religion": that they believed "in a future state of rewards and punishments." When Cohen, in the 1840s, was elected president of the council, the *Baltimore Patriot* commented that "it will no doubt be gratifying for our citizens to know that they have one filling the post, so eminently worthy of it, by previous long experience in the Councils, and by his general knowledge of the affairs of the city." To Isaac Lesser, publisher of *The Occident and American Jewish Advocate* in Philadelphia, Cohen's election proved "that a religious life as a professing Jew is no bar with enlightened Christians to appreciate merit and talent in an Israelite, and this, too, in a state where the removal of civil disabilities for opinions' sake is but of recent origin."[49]

Still, religious liberty was far from an accomplished fact in Maryland. "I have seen the first of my wishes as a public servant gratified," Kennedy announced, "by seeing the principles of civil and religious liberty established in the United States, and in seeing persecuted Children of Israel placed on an equality with their fellow citizens." But the "universal" bill Kennedy actually favored, with no religious tests, had been put aside in favor of a "specific" version for Jews only. Colonel Worthington claimed that the distinction between the bills did not matter, because there were "no followers of the koran, nor the zenda vesta, nor the morals of Confucius, nor the shaster [*sic*] of the Brahmins" in Maryland, "so that the only people it practically affects, are the followers of Moses." Any citizen who could not or would not accept Jewish or Christian theology remained barred from office. Generations more would pass before Maryland's law finally conformed to that of the United States Constitution.[50]

"Sleeping Thunder" in North Carolina

North Carolina was the penultimate state of the original thirteen to grant Jews political equality. Despite the example of other states, public pressures, and appeals by Jews and non-Jews to reverse the restrictive provisions of the 1776 constitution, the law remained unchanged for nearly a century. What was initially a theoretical concern in 1776, as no Jews then resided permanently in North Carolina, became a practical issue as handfuls of Jews drifted into the state in the decades following the American Revolution. The son of one such couple, Jacob Henry, born and raised in Carteret County, was elected to represent that county in the House of Commons. He served in the 1808 session without objection, possibly because no one noticed that he did not take the oath, or because no one recalled the constitutional prohibition. The following year, however, when Henry was reelected and seated, a delegate from Rockingham County, Hugh C. Mills, rose to protest. Mills demanded that Henry's seat be vacated on the ground that he "denies the divine authority of the New Testament, and refused to take the oath prescribed by law for his qualification."[51]

Henry was a Federalist, Mills a Republican. The strongest support for Henry came from a fellow Federalist and Catholic, William Gaston. Despite the clear words of Article 32 of the state constitution, that "no person, who shall deny the being of God or the truth of the Protestant religion" shall hold state office, Catholics had done so for some time without public objection. Catholics, moreover, took the required oath. As Gaston reasoned, he did not "deny" the truth of the Protestant religion; he simply did not "affirm" it. Henry could have utilized the same semantic loophole; but as a Jew he could not swear on "the divine authority" of the New Testament.[52]

Mills's attack came without warning, and overnight Henry composed an address that was later reprinted in several nineteenth-century collections of outstanding American oratory. He argued that the North Carolina Declaration of Rights included religious freedom as a "natural and unalienable right" guaranteed to all mankind, and that this guarantee took precedence over any other provisions of the state constitution that might be repugnant to it. Religion was "a question between a man and his Maker," and "no person, in this our land of liberty, has a right to arraign him at the bar of any inquisition." Henry conceded that anyone holding "religious principles incompatible with the freedom and safety of the State" should be barred from office, but he quickly added that he could not identify any known religious principles "which are thus dangerous"; certainly not Judaism. His creed "inculcates every duty which man owes to his fellow men; it enjoins upon its votaries, the practice of every virtue, and the detestation of every vice; it teaches them to hope for the favor of Heaven exactly in proportion as their lives are directed by just, honorable, and beneficent maxims." Henry spoke with deep feeling of his religion: "It was impressed upon my infant mind, it has been the director of my youth, the monitor of my manhood, and will I trust be the consolation of my old age." He concluded by saying that he did not know the religious beliefs "of those who have made this objection against me," or even if they had any, nor did it matter so long as "their actions are upright and their conduct just." It was not unreasonable to expect "the same charity . . . will be extended to myself, because in all things that relate to the State and to the duties of civil life, I am bound by the same obligations with my fellow citizens." [53]

The legislature found his argument persuasive—up to a point. Henry was permitted to retain his seat on the ground that legislators were not members of a "civil department within this State" and thus were exempt from the oath. At first glance the ruling appears strained if not farfetched, but in fact the United States Senate a decade earlier, in the William Blount case, dismissed impeachment charges against him on the same ground: that congressmen were not "civil officers of the United States." [54] The result was odd. Jews in North Carolina could be elected to the legislature, they could participate in making the laws of the state, but they were forbidden to hold any office executing or interpreting those laws.

The religious prohibitions of the North Carolina constitution became a dead issue in subsequent decades, except when conventions were held. Movements to revise the fundamental law in other respects, such as representation, apportionment, taxation, and internal improvements, invariably conjured up the ghost of Article 32. Thus, in 1823, at the stillborn "Western Convention" in Raleigh, Henry W. Harrington of Richmond County proposed that Article 32 be expunged as hostile to the liberality of the age and to the principles of religious freedom. The president of the convention, Bartlett Yancy, suggested that it be withdrawn as a subject foreign to the objects of their meeting. Harrington reluctantly obliged. A decade later a committee of the legislature, preparing substitute recommendations to specific portions of the constitution, reported that "the 32nd article should be abolished, at least in part, if not altogether. Its spirit is in conflict with Religious freedom; it has no practical use; and it may be considered a mere badge of ancient prejudice, which, however excusable in those who first engrafted it upon our Constitution, is unworthy the present age of enlightened liberty." The general assembly approved the motion, which followed the committee report, fifty to nine.[55]

But when a constitutional convention met in Raleigh in 1835, the outcome was different. None of the problems that the delegates confronted aroused more debate or consumed more time than Article 32, the so-called meaningless relic. Two delegates rose from their sickbeds to speak and to vote on the issue. More than two dozen delegates felt obliged to deliver orations (their lengthy speeches take up a third of the convention journal). Some wished to keep the original provision intact, others to remove it entirely; but the largest majority voted to replace the word "Protestant" with the word "Christian," thus maintaining a restriction against Jews and atheists. That majority was made up of those who believed it was the best compromise attainable, that at least some progress had been made, and by those who insisted that they could not vote otherwise because it reflected the overwhelming sentiment of their constituents. There were few Jews in the state, and no publicly admitted atheists, yet the delegates felt bound to protect posterity from the potential threat of non-Christians.

An analysis of their votes reveals no significant difference based upon the delegates' religious denomination or geographical location. William Gaston, the most prominent Catholic in the state and a leader of the Whig party, delivered the longest and most learned disquisition, touching upon legal, historical, and philosophical points to support a motion to end all religious tests. Article 32, he argued, may not have

> kept out of the public service any individual who might have
> otherwise entered into it—but it does not thence follow that no
> practical evil has arisen from it. If it has impaired the attachment
> of any citizen to the institutions of his country, by causing him
> to feel that a stigma was cast, or attempted to be cast, upon him,
> in its fundamental law; if it has swelled the arrogance or em
> bittered the malice of sectarian bigotry by bidding it hold up its
> head on high above the suspected castes of the community; if it
> has checked the fair expression of honest opinion, or operated as
> a bribe to hypocrisy and dissimulation . . . then, vast indeed,
> has already been its practical mischief. But had it produced
> none—this would be a very insufficient apology for retaining it.

Dead is it? Then is it fit for cleanly riddance. Then let us inter the carcass, lest its pestilential effluvia should poison the atmosphere of freedom.[56]

Nathaniel Macon, respected for his long service to the Democratic party and his national reputation, and who was elected president of the convention, agreed with Gaston. Article 32, he said, "was the only feature in the old Constitution which he had ever heard objected to out of the State." A nominal Baptist and unalloyed Jeffersonian, Macon shocked many listeners by stating that "if a Hindoo were to come among us, and was fully qualified to discharge the duties of any office to which he might aspire, his religious belief would not constitute an objection, in his opinion, why he should be debarred. Who made man a judge, that he should presume to interfere in the sacred rights of conscience?"[57]

"The venerable Macon and the eloquent Gaston have fought shoulder to shoulder," the Norfolk *Beacon* commented.[58] But their views were in a distinct minority. John Motley Morehead of Guilford County objected to the implied slurs upon the memory of the Presbyterian minister, the Reverend David Caldwell, who had labored in 1776 for the inclusion of Article 32. "There never was a truer Whig than Dr. Caldwell, nor one that had the good of his country more at heart," stated Morehead, who wanted no change.[59] Nor did a Moravian (United Brethren) delegate, Gottlieb Shober: "It has been a part of our Constitution for 50 years—it has stood as a beacon to aspirants for office, as an axiom that we prize Religion, and tells the world we are a Christian people. Call it superstition if you please, yet it appears to me it is that kind of superstition which tends to strengthen our free institutions." Jesse Cooper of Martin County claimed that "in his section there was not one gentleman in a hundred that wanted this Article touched." Charles Fisher of Rowan County—the leader of the western wing of the Democratic party—advised the convention not to "give up *practical good* through fears of *ideal evils*." James Smith of Orange County agreed that Article 32 should be kept as "Sleeping Thunder" to be used when necessary. He "was not willing, by expunging this Article, to let in Turks, Hindoos, and Jews. They might call him a bigot as much as they pleased, but he would not consent to this. In what way could we bind them to a proper discharge of their duties if we should admit them? Must we swear a Turk on the Koran? Must we separate the Holy Scriptures that we must swear the Jew on the Old Testament?"[60]

A motion declaring that "all religious tests, as qualifications for office, are incompatible with the principles of free government" lost, eighty-seven to thirty-six. A motion withholding office only from those who denied the existence of God lost, eighty-two to forty-two. Reworded somewhat, it lost seventy-eight to forty-seven. Again reworded, it lost eighty to forty-six. A move to strike the words "or who shall hold religious principles incompatible with the freedom and safety of the State," lost eighty-seven to thirty-nine. A majority of the delegates appeared to be willing to make one concession, however, to strike the word "Protestant" for the word "Christian." "If we cannot make room for the Jew, if he be thought worthy of office," Samuel Carson of Burke County argued, "let us not refuse the privilege for Christians of every denomination." John Branch, ex-governor of the state, disagreed. "Why are the Jews to be excluded from office?" he asked. "They were the favorite people of the Almighty. Our Savior and His disciples were Jews, and are there not men among the Jews as talented, as virtuous, as well qualified to fill any office in our Government as any other citizen in our Community? A Jew may be appointed to any office under the General Government. He may be raised to the Presidency of the United States, and why shall we refuse to admit him to any office under our government?" Jesse Wilson, a Quaker delegate from Perquimons County, also pleaded the Jewish cause: "Who is prepared to say that there is not at this very moment among us, some son of Abraham who, fired by genius and prompted by the most laudable ambition, may, in the course of the next thirty years, by dint of his extraordinary talents, cultivated and nurtured by the most studious and unremitted industry, occupy the topmost place in the affections of the State. Is it unlikely?"[61]

Despite similar speeches, the compromise passed, seventy-four to fifty-one. A majority of both eastern and western delegates supported the measure. By party, seventy-two percent of the Whigs voted in its favor, and sixty-three percent of the Democrats were in opposition; although some of the latter—such as Branch and Wilson—did so on principle, because they were against all religious tests.[62] "It was hoped, indeed we believe it was the intention of the people that this [religious] distinction should be done away by the Convention," commented the *Newbern Spectator*, "but a majority of the members thought it better to retain the spirit of the odious restriction on liberty of conscience, notwithstanding the brilliant and convincing arguments used by Judge Gaston and other distinguished gentlemen in favor of a more liberal course."[63] Gaston, in fact, voted for the compromise.

Twenty years later, in 1855, when the Jews of Wilmington dedicated their own burying ground, Isaac Leeser of Philadelphia was invited to speak at the services, which were attended by an audience of Jews and Christians. He used the opportunity to appeal for a change in the law. "In death all are alike" said Leeser,

> but while the burden of earthly existence is on us, the son of Israel is excluded from equal rights by the constitution which governs you as the supreme law. This is not well; it is a disgrace to a state, in this age of the world, to exclude any one for the sake of the opinions he entertains, regarding his idea of the God-head and the religious duties which he thinks himself bound to observe. . . . I will, therefore, appeal to all who now hear me, to all who have any weight or influence among their fellow citizens, to exert their power to aid in wiping out this blot, this disgrace from the escutcheon of North Carolina; yes, labor faithfully and unweariedly until the constitution of your state be freed from that stain of the anomalous clause which throws the mantle of equal protection on all the citizens, excepting only those who adhere to the faith of Israel.[64]

Leeser repeated this message in his newspaper, *The Occident*, and kept up a correspondence with North Carolina Jews, urging them to action. Petitions addressed to the legislature were circulated "to remove from the fundamental law of the State this last remnant of bigotry and prejudice," and the *Wilmington Journal* supported the attempt: "We do not care for commencing any agitation or starting any new issue. We merely state our opinion that the invidious distinction in our State Constitution against the members of this religious denomination is not in accordance with the liberal spirit of the age in which we live. The number of Israelites in North Carolina is very small, and does not to our knowledge and belief, contain a single man who is an applicant for office of any kind, and therefore the incapacity for holding it is more invidious because wholly gratuitous." In 1858 a bill to remove the constitutional clause that "prohibited persons of the Jewish or Israeltish faith from holding offices of profit or trust in this State" was referred to a judiciary committee of the legislature. The committee reported that the purpose of the bill was well founded, that the clause represented "a relic of bigotry and intolerance unfit to be associated in our fundamental law with the enlightened principles of representative government," but they recommended against its passage: "it is highly inexpedient at this time to alter or amend the Constitution by legislative enactment in any particular whatever." Once again the *Wilmington Journal* was critical: "This is not a matter which concerns simply the few persons of the Jewish faith within our borders. It is a matter which concerns the reputation of the State of North Carolina. Shall it be said that her people will perpetuate a proscriptive feature of their Constitution which is . . . condemned by all generous minds? Surely not."[65]

A number of North Carolina Jews, signing themselves "Several Israelites," addressed a note "TO THE CANDIDATES FOR THE STATE LEGISLATURE," asking each one, "Will you, if elected, use your influence to remove the odious disability clause in the Constitution, which excludes the Jewish citizens of the State from holding offices of profit and trust?" When no replies were received, S. A. Cohen of Charlotte, in the *Charlotte Bulletin*, asked the candidates if they feared "committing themselves before the illiberal and biassed few opposed to Judaism? A few such minds will be found in every country; but the time will come when knowledge will teach that wrong can never be right, as the Judiciary Committee tried to make us believe at the last session of the legislature." The editor of the *Bulletin* appended a note of agreement, hoping that "Governor [John W.] Ellis will meet the question squarely . . . and grant, by his expression of sentiment, full and equal rights to all good citizens, whether they be Protestants, Romanists, or Jews."[66] The legislature did nothing. A Mr. Crumpler, a delegate from Ashe County, made an anti-Semitic speech, accusing Jews of cheating, of dealing unfairly, of being mere consumers, living off the labors of others. "One of the Reviled," (probably S. A. Cohen), answered Crumpler in the *Charlotte Bulletin*, ending his letter with a promise that Jews would live by the law, unjust as it was, and a commitment of loyalty to the state despite the law. "Should she need the services of her sons in the present crisis," he wrote, "Jews will be found among those battling for her rights and institutions."[67]

When a convention that assembled in Raleigh in 1861 voted to secede and to join the Confederacy and then proceeded to revise the state

constitution, no substantive change was made on the question of religious qualifications for holding office. Thomas Ruffin, who had served
as chief justice of the state, had been a friend and supporter of William
Gaston decades earlier. In 1832 Ruffin informed Gaston, "I am very
decidedly persuaded, and have long been, that Roman Catholics cannot, without giving to the terms of the Constitution a latitude and force
altogether unauthorized, be excluded from civil office."[68] The same
apparently did not apply to Jews, and in 1861 Ruffin made sure it
would not by introducing a motion to continue the ancient prohibition
against non-Christians. The convention approved Ruffin's motion,
eighty-four to twenty-two. Asa Biggs, who also had a distinguished
political career, having served in both houses of the national Congress
from North Carolina and as a United States district court judge, introduced a contrary motion to end all religious tests for holding office in
the new constitution. It was defeated sixty-nine to thirty-three. The
convention then approved a final ordinance incorporating Ruffin's motion, ninety-six to nine. There was no debate. Even Biggs voted in the
affirmative.[69]

Four years of fighting for their native state did not help the Jews of
North Carolina. The convention that met in October 1865, called in
pursuance of President Andrew Johnson's plan of reconstruction, kept
the old religious oath that barred Jews from office. Not until 1868, at
the convention called under the "radical" congressional plan of reconstruction—at which none of the old white leadership of North Carolina
was present—was the oath abolished. Not a single voice opposed removing the disqualifications. Only those who "shall deny the Being of
Almighty God" remained barred.[70]

*The issue followed the frontier line, erupting periodically for more
than a century. It was raised again and again, although not in all
states, and not always at the initial constitutional conventions: Should
there be a recognition of Christianity in the fundamental law, reflect-
ing a Christian population, or should the secular example of the federal Constitution be followed? Thus, in Kentucky, late in the eighteenth century, where the liberal influence of Virginia predominated,
an anticlerical spirit easily carried the day. "Theologues," writing in
the* Kentucky Gazette, *urged that Protestantism be the test for "any
place of trust, or profit, in either the civil or military department of the*

state." *Another writer, disagreeing with him, suggested that member-ship in a particular church was unimportant as long as the officer "is reported to be devout, sincere, and faithful to the religion he does pro-fess. But a loose liver, or an apostate in religion, I cannot think fit to be trusted in the state, because a man who is not true to his God, will not probably be so to his country."*[71] *In the end Kentucky adopted religious liberty clauses patterned closely after Jefferson's statute of religious liberty.*

In Tennessee, on the other hand, the strong Presbyterian example of North Carolina was manifest. There the religious issue had been de-bated during the unsuccessful attempt to form the state of Franklin—the predecessor to Tennessee—in the 1780s. A decade later, when an-other convention met in Knoxville to fashion a constitution, it was again debated. The proposed bill of rights declared "that no religious test shall ever be required as a qualification to any office of public trust under this State." The body of the proposed constitution stated exactly the opposite: "No person who publicly denies the being of a God, and future rewards and punishments, or the divine authority of the old and new testaments, shall hold any office in the civil department of this state." Those who supported the aborted "Houston constitution" of the 1780s wanted the Christian restrictions maintained. Their oppo-nents, led by William Blount, succeeded by the narrowest margin in having a key phrase—the reference to the scriptures—deleted. (It should be noted that the Blount forces voted against eliminating the entire clause.) One Presbyterian who attended the convention and who because of his background would be assumed to support the Christian profession of faith—Andrew Jackson—in fact "opposed it," according to his biographer, and played "a prominent role in fighting it, and suc-ceeded in winning the deletion of its final section.[72]

A century of expansion changed the face of America but not the issue of a Christian constitution as opposed to a secular one. The speaker of the House of Representatives in California, William W. Stow, sug-gested in 1855 that "the Bible lay at the foundation of our institutions, and its ordinances ought to be covered and adhered to in legislating for this state." He favored "inflicting such a tax" upon Jews "as would act as a prohibition to their residence amongst us." A storm of protest followed. Stow's remarks were widely criticized, although in Sacra-mento, dissatisfied with the editorials in the local newspaper, Jews

were forced to publish their lengthy rebuttal as a paid advertise-
ment (under the heading "His Holiness King Stow vs. the Jews of
California").[73]

The creation of a National Reform Association during the Civil War
(see chapter 3) served to spur the attempt to Christianize constitutions.
When the Colorado convention met in 1876, for example, religious
questions dominated its meetings. Catholics from the southern part of
the state and Protestants from the north argued bitterly over the taxa-
tion of church property, school appropriations, and the reading of the
Bible in public schools.[74] *Whether the preamble to the proposed state*
constitution should contain a reference to God, or to a specific God,
according to the Denver Daily Tribune, *"agitated the people of Colo-*
rado more than any other matter."[75] *One delegate reasoned that the*
United States Constitution seemed to function well enough without
mention of a divinity. Opponents warned that Colorado citizens would
reject a document that failed to recognize God.

Fifty-six "citizens of the Territory" signed a petition requesting that
"no privilege or advantage shall be conceded to Christianity or any
other special religion," and "that our entire political system shall be
founded and administered on a purely secular basis." Presbyterian
fundamentalists submitted a contrary petition requesting that God be
identified as Jesus Christ, and that the constitution should acknowl-
edge the truth of the Old and New Testament:

> *We, the undersigned, do respectfully petition your honorable*
> *body to incorporate in the preamble of the constitution of the*
> *State of Colorado, to be presented to the people for their adop-*
> *tion, a suitable recognition of Almighty God as the author of*
> *national existence, and the source of all power and authority in*
> *civil government; of Jesus Christ as the ruler of nations, and of*
> *the Bible as the fountain of law and supreme rule for the con-*
> *duct of nations.*[76]

Both petitions were disregarded, and Colorado settled for a non-
denominational reference in its constitution. The preamble merely
stated a "profound reverence for the Supreme Ruler of the Universe."
In so deciding it followed the example of states that were added to the
union after the original thirteen. None recognized the divinity of Christ
or prohibited non-Protestants from holding office. This fact does not
mean that the issue disappeared.

We Are a Christian Nation

The right to hold office was not the only issue that preoccupied American Jews. Their vigilance extended to rooting out any discrimination that had the sanction of law or policy. Thus, a marriage law in Georgia, an incorporation law in the District of Columbia, and a law of evidence in Maryland, to name a few, which favored Christians, were eliminated as the result of Jewish protests.[1] When governors, sometimes unwittingly, placed an explicitly Christian rather than a nonsectarian identification into their Thanksgiving Day proclamations, Jews again protested—with various results.[2]

Catholics, of course, did not object to Christian identifications or laws favoring Christians. But they labored against some of the same official and quasi-official discriminations as did the Jews. Both were victims of bigotry, the Catholics more so when nativism reached its apogee by the mid-nineteenth century. Jews, for historical and practical reasons, were tempted to join the nativist crusade—and some succumbed. But most Jewish leaders recognized that religious equality was fundamental to their position. It could not be compromised. Moreover, they realized that the foremost threat to their interest came from the nativists who would deny equality to all non-Protestants.

The Mortara Case

A number of Jewish spokesmen abandoned the doctrine of religious equality and in fact joined in nativist attacks upon Catholics. Perhaps the most rabid was Lewis C. Levin, originally from South Carolina, who played a prominent role in the anti-Catholic riots in Philadelphia in 1844 and then served as a Native American representative to Congress for three years. An energetic but somewhat unstable fanatic, consumed with hatred of Catholics and foreigners, Levin drifted into insanity. Before his death in 1860 he accused Republicans and abolitionists of being agents of the pope.[3] Jewish-Catholic relations had been prickly from the beginning, and their examples of cooperation (as in Maryland, over the "Jew bill") had been laced with suspicions. Both were minorities. Both were overwhelmingly Democratic in political affiliation. Both were hostile to abolitionism and usually avoided any radicalism that might have affected their acceptance as Americans. Both suffered the same kinds of internal stresses, usually between older settlers and recent immigrants. Indeed, many of their individual churches adopted Protestant fashions, with Catholics holding emotional religious revivals, and Jews singing hymns to organ music.[4] (A New York City *Evening Post* reporter attending a Jewish service at Temple Emmanuel commented, "One might think himself in a Ritualist church during the 'Gloria,' except for the omission of the usual sign of the cross.")[5] Yet despite their mutual interests and examples of cooperation, Jews and Catholics fundamentally distrusted one another. Shortly before the Civil War an open hostility flared. A sensational incident in the Papal States, the seizure by Catholics of a seven-year-old Jewish child, ordered by the archbishop of Bologna (on the grounds that the child, Edgar Mortara, had been secretly baptized by a Catholic servant), led to an international outcry in England, Europe, and the United States.

"Agitate without ceasing in conjunction with protestant Christians," an Episcopalian lawyer publicly advised Philadelphia Jews.[6] The advice was superfluous. Jewish congregations throughout the nation held meetings to decide upon a course of action. Resolutions were passed and letters of protest sent, which were sometimes contradictory in nature, to Secretary of State Lewis Cass and to President James Buchanan. Mass assemblies in New York City and in San Francisco attracted thousands of Jews and Protestants, with lesser numbers meeting in other cities all across America. Virtually the entire Protestant press and, with some exceptions, the secular press voiced their indignation. (All Catholic papers defended the legality and morality of the abduction.)

The Know-Nothing party, which was almost defunct by this time, tried in vain to capitalize upon the Mortara case in order to restore itself. The Sachem of the Order of United Americans wrote a public letter to a Jewish member of that order reminding him that "Webster defines the word 'Protestant' as '*one who protests against Popery.*' Now surely there is *no sect* of the whole human race that has a *greater reason to protest against Popery* than the Israelites." The leader of the Baltimore Know-Nothings, Congressman James M. Harris, tried to introduce a resolution in the national House of Representatives asking the president to intercede to free Mortara. Know-Nothing speakers appeared at public meetings with other Protestants and Jews, and in Albany there was open and active cooperation between Jews and nativists.[7] Rabbi Isaac M. Wise recalled being bitterly attacked by "a number of Jews" for criticizing the Know-Nothing party. One member of his congregation, "like other American aristocrats," stated that she favored a suggested nativist law by which foreigners could obtain citizenship only after a residence of twenty-one years.[8]

Although most Jews were careful to disassociate their views from the Know-Nothing nativists and in fact either were honestly concerned with or paid lip service to the idea of religious equality, the anti-Catholic theme remained paramount. "Thank Heaven we live in the United States, where no Catholic would dare to kidnap or abduct one of our children," wrote Rabbi Samuel Isaacs in the *Jewish Messenger*. But the leaders of the Jewish community in Saint Louis were not so sure. There a Jew, Captain Paulson Dietrich, who was dying in a Catholic hospital, had been isolated from visitors, baptized without his consent, and buried in a Catholic cemetery. Only after considerable agitation was the body disinterred and reburied according to Jewish ritual in a Jewish cemetery. In a letter to the secretary of state, the Saint Louis congregation warned that because all priests recognized papal supremacy, acts "similar" to the Mortara case "will occur in the United States." The *New York Times* concurred: "If *rascally servants* may clandestinely baptize the children of Hebrews, there is no reason why they should not extend the same blessing to those of Protestants." So did the Philadelphia *Presbyterian*: "It is absurd to expect that our own country is to be exempt from this new method, if it is indeed a new method, of proselytism." Another Presbyterian paper cautioned its readers that their children were endangered any time "a Popish nurse happens to throw a little water on its face." And a Chicago paper agreed that the Mortara case "places the children of all parents not Catholic entirely at the mercy of the Inquisition."[9]

In San Francisco Rabbi Julius Eckman cautioned the audience to distinguish between "Catholics and Catholicism," but a Protestant speaker, F. P. Tracy, did not follow that advice: "The pope would baptize every one of us, if he only had the power. Should they increase upon us, God only knows what the end will be." In Chicago a Protestant alderman declared that "the horrors of the Inquisition are still fresh in the memory of the civilized world." In Albany a rabbi referred to the "insidious Jesuits" and invited his listeners to "closely and unitedly watch every step of the Roman Catholic Church." A Protestant minister from Cumberland, Ohio, Matthew R. Miller, claimed that "the little Hebrew boy Edgar Mortara has *passively* given the world one of the best arguments of all the nineteenth century against Popery." Voices of moderation were not silent but could scarcely be heard above the shrill denunciations of papal plots and Catholic cruelties exemplified by this "monstrous crime against God and humanity." Perhaps the only light note was struck by a Jewish speaker, Raphael De Cordova.

> Supposing the child had been baptized clandestinely by a nurse, did that make him a Catholic? Let them reverse the case and suppose a band of armed Jews were to penetrate into the Vatican—seize upon the Pope, and with a razor or some other sharp instrument (universal tittering), were to perform the operation of circumcision upon the person of that holy man (uproarious laughter), surely that would not make the Pope a Jew, any more than the sprinkling of water made a child of a Jew a Christian. But what, think you, would be the opinion of His Holiness on such a "miracle as that."[10]

The Mortara case inevitably became a political issue. Democrats defended the administration's course of nonintervention in the internal affairs of another country. Rabbi Isaac Wise protested this policy. He wrote to Senator Stephen A. Douglas, warning him that the "Democratic Party is too much identified with Jesuitism and Catholicism, a fact which estranges to her the liberal class of the northern population." Jews, he claimed, were being "frightened away" from their traditional party allegiance.[11] Republicans, of course, attempted to turn a political profit by attracting the Jewish vote. They declared it to be a "sacred duty" of the federal government to intervene lest, as a San Francisco newspaper commented, Irish chambermaids might baptize "half the infants in the United States." One of Lincoln's political advisors, Abraham Jonas, suggested to Senator Lyman Trumbull that the Jewish vote could be won over.

> Here in Illinois we have no chance in the world for the Catholic vote. The Jewish abduction case at Rome is making a considerable stir among the Israelites here and among the liberal and free thinking Germans and also among the *Know-Nothings.* Could you not introduce some Resolution into the Senate on the subject and get the Republican vote for it. . . . It will make in this county a change of 100 votes, and unite the Jewish vote all over the Union. In the free states there are 50,000 Jewish votes, two-thirds of whom vote the Democratic ticket. I conversed yesterday with an intelligent German Jew from Cincinnati who is a Democrat—he is satisfied that 1,000 votes in that city would be brought over to the Republican side if the course suggested by me could be adopted.[12]

A growing number of Jews were or did become Republican, particularly in the Midwest, but the large majority remained firmly in the Democratic fold, as did the Catholics. Jewish-Catholic relations continued poor. In 1860, when the House of Representatives took up a suggestion by Schuyler Colfax of Indiana and invited a rabbi (for the first time) to open its session with prayers, the editor of a Catholic newspaper in Baltimore commented that it was "monstrous" in a Christian country to choose a Jew to pray in the national councils. Isaac Leeser responded that "Catholicism . . . has extended [itself] almost wonderfully in America, notwithstanding that my people are [their] equals," and that it was high time indeed for Jews to be *"publicly* exhibited as [their] equals in the Halls of Congress."[13]

Not Catholicism, however, but nativism, was the major threat to Jewish interests, a fact that was understood by the more thoughtful

Jewish leaders. As early as 1853 Jonathan Nathan confided to Hamilton Fish, former governor of New York, that he was "particularly sensitive on Native Americanism and religious intolerance."[14] Philip Phillips, a congressman from Alabama, wrote a public letter in 1855 to the editor of the *Mobile Register* that excoriated the Know-Nothing party. Its national platform stated that "Christianity, by the constitution of nearly all the States, by the decisions of the most eminent judicial authorities, and by the consent of the people of America, is considered *an element of our political system.*" Phillips rebutted that argument and reminded readers "how smoothly the inference is drawn" by nativists "that a pure Christianity requires the exclusion of Catholics from the rights of citizenship." Religious intolerance, Phillips noted,

> is as old as the history of man. In this country, where freedom
> and equality, under the shadow of the law, walk hand in hand
> throughout the land, intolerance lies dormant in the breast, or,
> when excited into action, shrinks from the public eye. [The
> Know-Nothing party] is the first in the history of our country
> which has dared openly to stimulate this feeling for political ob-
> jects: thus, in the name of Christianity itself, laying the train to
> light the torch of religious persecution.[15]

Nativism as a separate political movement declined markedly by the Civil War, but nativism as an emotion had not, and the uproar over the Mortara case served to spur it on. The strange alliance of some Jews joining in the anti-Catholic outburst could not mask the core of the message of the nativists: that Protestant Christianity was "*an element of our political system.*" From that message it was an easy step for nativists to revive an idea that Jews dreaded, to amend the Constitution to recognize the divinity of Jesus Christ.

The Christian Amendment

The idea certainly was not new. When the ratification of the Constitution was debated there had been numerous complaints that an acknowledgment of Christ had not been included in the fundamental law of the land. Thereafter, periodically, various ministers regretted the omission. In his published notes to a sermon that he delivered in 1793, the Reverend John M. Mason of New York wrote,

That no notice whatever should be taken of that God who planteth a nation and plucketh it up at His pleasure, is an omission which no pretext whatever can palliate. Had such a momentous business been transacted by Mohammedans, they would have begun, 'In the name of God.' Even the savages whom we despise, setting a better example, would have paid some homage to the Great Spirit. But from the Constitution of the United States, it is impossible to ascertain what God we worship, or whether we own a God at all. . . . Should the citizens of America be as irreligious as her Constitution, we will have reason to tremble, lest the Governor of the universe, who will not be treated with indignity by a people any more than by individuals, overturn from its foundations the fabric we have been rearing, and crush us to atoms in the wreck.[16]

The Reverend Samuel Austin, later president of the University of Vermont, warned his congregation in 1811 that the Constitution "is entirely disconnected from Christianity. It is not founded on the Christian religion." This "one capital defect" would lead "inevitably to its destruction." Without Christian rulers, the Reverend Jedidiah Morse predicted, in 1812, America was doomed. As Israel was punished, so would be America. The Reverend Samuel Taggart, who represented Hampshire, Massachusetts, in Congress, called the omission of Christ from the Constitution "a national evil of great magnitude." "Be astonished, O earth!" repeated another minister, Chauncey Lee, "the Constitution has not the impress of religion upon it, not the smallest recognition of the government being of God. . . . I leave [the subject] with this single reflection, whether if God be not in the camp, we have not reason to tremble for the ark?"[17]

The theme was repeated over and over again: The United States was imperiled by a Constitution that not only failed to honor God but permitted non-Christians or non-Protestants to hold office. At Carlisle, Pennsylvania, in 1819, the Reverend George Duffield declared it "a great sin to have forgotten God in such an important national instrument, and not to have acknowledged Him in that which forms the very nerves and sinews of the political body." The Reverend James Wilson, chaplain of the New York legislature, stated in 1820 that the founding fathers displayed "a degree of ingratitude, perhaps without a parallel," in forming a Constitution "in which there is not the slightest hint of homage to the God of Heaven." [18] In a famous sermon preached in 1827, the Reverend Ezra Stiles Ely argued, "We are a Christian nation: we have the right to demand that all our rulers in their conduct shall conform to Christian morality; and if they do not, it is the duty of Christian freemen to make a new and a better election." [19] The initial fault, and the source of many national problems, resided in the Constitution. "It is negatively *atheistical*, for no God is appealed to at all," wrote the Reverend D. X. Junkin in 1845. "In framing many of our public formularies, greater care seems to have been taken to adapt them to the prejudices of the INFIDEL FEW, than to the consciences of the Christian millions." [20]

These periodic laments were isolated and did not disturb Jews unduly. They were in the main the work of religious zealots who could not be taken seriously. Surely the majority of Americans did not subscribe to the idea of a Christian amendment that would have doomed the separation of church and state. Thus, in 1861, when the members of a Presbyterian synod in Allegheny, Pennsylvania, composed a petition deploring the absence of Christ or his laws from the Constitution "as wholly inconsistent with all claims to be considered a Christian nation or to enjoy the protection and favor of God," Jews registered a mild concern. True, their petition was submitted to Congress by an important senator, Charles Sumner. And two members of the synod, the Reverend J. R. W. Sloane of New York and the Reverend A. M. Milligan of Pennsylvania, journeyed to Washington and presented their petitions to President Abraham Lincoln. [21] But as the Reverend Matthew R. Miller, himself a Presbyterian minister, noted in a letter to *The Occident*,

> The Synod represented one of the smallest families of Presbyterianism. It was a Synod of those who call themselves "Reformed Presbyterians" and who are commonly designated by the name "Covenanters". . . . They never cast a vote at any election if the successful candidate must swear to support the Constitution of the United States. While the Constitution makes no reference to Jesus as supreme king, and to the Bible as supreme law, they pronounce it infidel. [22]

Miller was wrong, however. Precisely what Jews always feared, an ecumenical movement of Protestants to define America as a Christian nation, appeared to be growing in strength. Jewish leaders displayed no interest in Protestant theological disagreements, so long as those disagreements continued. "We will not advert to the different sects of Christians, who all claim to be the correct interpreters of the gospel," Isaac Leeser commented. "As far as we are concerned they are all alike."[23] But from 1861 to 1863, from moderates as well as from fundamentalists of many Protestant denominations, came a call to put God in the Constitution of the United States. The Reverend Horace Bushnell of Connecticut, following the battle of Bull Run, preached a sermon, "Reverses Needed," in which he argued that out of the "long, weary, terrible sacrifices" of war would arise, for the first time, a true nationality grounded in spiritual suffering shared by all Americans. Hitherto we had been a nation in name only. Bushnell blamed the founding fathers for establishing a government without moral or religious ideas, based upon "godless theorizing." How could there be loyalty without a spiritual foundation? How could there be patriotic devotion to an instrument that failed to recognize that all authority is derived from God? The fighting, the sacrifices, the inevitable victory, however, would generate "a kind of religious crowning of our nationality. All the atheistic jargon we have left behind us will be gone." Bushnell suggested that "it might not be amiss, at some fit time," to add a recognition of God's authority in the preamble to the Constitution. By doing this we would succeed in "cutting off . . . the false theories under which we have been so fatally demoralized."[24]

A New York City church paper, *The Independent*, probably the most influential religious publication in the country, published an editorial agreeing with Bushnell. "From this atheistic error in our prime conceptions of government," wrote the editors, "has arisen the atheistic habit of separating politics from religion," the error of worshipping the work of one's own hands rather than that of God. Even in the national legislature, "when Senators are warned that a measure is unjust and against the law of God, it is sneeringly, scornfully answered, 'There is no higher law than the Constitution.'"[25]

Bushnell was not a Protestant fundamentalist—he had long broken with the evangelical alliance—but as a leading theologian, his sermon aided their cause. Bushnell spoke of God's absence from the Constitution; the fundamentalists defined God as Christ, more specifically a Protestant Christ. The Civil War, so it seemed to thousands of religious Americans, was God's punishment, not only because of slavery, but because He was omitted from the Constitution. "For more than forty years, a Fourth of July has seldom passed," wrote the Reverend George Junkin of Lafayette College, in 1863, "on which I have not preached and warned my countrymen of this defect, and told them if it be not supplied, God would pull down their temple and bury a nation in its ruins." The Reverend Henry A. Boardman of Philadelphia argued that "the loss of His favor will explain everything that has happened." Only by placing Christ in the Constitution could it be regained. The Reverend Robert J. Breckenridge wrote in the *Danville Review* that "we are reaping the effects of its implied atheism."[26] (In the South, though less often, the necessity of Christianizing the Confederate government became a pulpit subject. At the funeral for John Hemphill, for example, the Reverend Moses Hoge referred to the deceased as "a Christian Statesman." Hoge remarked that Christianity is "the vitalizing force of a nation. . . . The Bible—emphatically the Word—the utterance of Divine Wisdom—should be the manual of the public man, the textbook of the statesman.")[27]

The long history of objections to the Constitution, now concentrated in hundreds of wartime sermons and pamphlets, led to the creation of an organization whose sole purpose was to place Christ in the Constitution. In February 1863, at Sparta, Illinois, a convention of clergymen resolved "to labor to bring the nation to repentance toward God, and to faithful administration of the government according to the principles of the word of God." They formed an association to carry out their resolution. Independent of the Sparta meetings, another convention, representing eleven denominations from seven states, met that same month at Xenia, Ohio, on the theme "The Revival of Religion." A Presbyterian layman, John Alexander, suggested that as a condition to the revival of religion in the nation, the Constitution should be amended to recognize "the rulership of Jesus Christ and the supremacy of the divine law." One witness recalled the debate that ensued: "A most vigorous discussion occupied the evening session, running until eleven o'clock at night. All the old objections of church and state, imposing on Jew and Atheist, and infringement on conscience, were threshed over, and also the sacredness and immutability of the Constitution, were pleaded as against any amendment of any kind." Emotions ran at a "fever pitch," and the chairman decided to permit the entire audience, rather than the official delegates, to vote on the question. "To the exceeding delight of the friends of [Alexander's] paper, the many hundreds crowding the body and galleries of that largest church of the city arose as one man in favor of it. . . . There was not a dissenting vote. The decision was so sweeping that opposing members of the convention seemed to lack the courage to put in a dissent."[28]

The organizational meetings that followed in Pittsburgh and in Philadelphia created the nondenominational National Reform Association, with John Alexander as its first president. Precisely how to word the amendment so as to neither offend nor favor any particular Protestant church occupied most of their attention. Should it refer to "Jesus the Messiah, the Savior and Lord of all," or "Jesus the Prince of Kings of the Earth," or should it make no special reference to Jesus? Professor J. H. McIlvaine of Princeton University believed general phrases such as "Almighty God" and "His revealed will" would suffice as a harmonious compromise that all Christians could support. Others complained that these words were too vague. The Reverend James M. Wilson stated that "he could go for nothing that does not make a distinct recognition of Jesus Christ through whom alone we can approach unto God." The meeting finally settled upon the following rewording of the preamble of the Constitution: "Recognizing Almighty God as the source of all authority and power in civil government, and acknowledging the Lord Jesus Christ as the Governor among the nations, His revealed will as the supreme law of the land, in order to constitute a Christian government. . . ."[29]

For Jews the formation of the National Reform Association was but one manifestation of what they saw as a rapid movement to Christianize the country officially. "ARE WE EQUALS IN THIS LAND?" *The Occident* queried in 1863.[30] North and South political leaders referred to the war as a Christian battle fought to preserve Christian principles. Many of the speeches, the songs, the prayers, the fast-day proclamations, and even the laws and military orders recognized the primacy of Christianity. In 1860 Congress had invited a rabbi to open its session with prayer. But a year later a new war-Congress passed a law requiring that all army chaplains "must be regularly ordained ministers of some Christian religion." They did not enact this measure without considering the Jews, because in debate Congressman Clement Vallandigham of Ohio—an opponent of the war—pointed out the discriminatory nature of the intended legislation.[31] It took complaints from a Jewish organization, the Board of Delegates of American Israelites, appeals to President Lincoln, and a number of petitions and memorials from Jews in several states to individual congressmen before the law was amended on 17 July 1862.

Nevertheless, four months later, on 15 November 1862, Lincoln issued an order in which he stated that due to "the sacred rights of Christian soldiers and sailors" and "deference to the best sentiment of a Christian people," all military commanders were to observe Sunday as a day of rest.[32] The distraught father of a Jewish soldier wrote to Lincoln: "I gave my consent to my son, who was yet a minor, that he should enlist. . . . I thought it was his duty, and I gave him my advice to fulfill his duty as a good citizen. At the same time I taught him to observe the Sabbath on Saturday, when it would not hinder him from fulfilling his duty in the army. Now I do not want that he shall be dragged either to the stake or the church to observe the Sunday as a Sabbath."[33]

More ominous for Jews was the burgeoning anti-semitism that seemed to expand as the war lengthened in time. North and South, Jews were accused of disloyalty and corruption. "The descendants of that accursed race who crucified the Savior," the Newburgh, New York, *Journal* editorialized, "are always opposed to the best interests of the government in every land in which they roam. [They] never enter our armies but for the purpose of depleting the pockets of soldiers."[34] In the Mississippi valley, according to one scholar, "virtually every diatribe delivered against [cotton] speculators by army officers or others . . . betrayed a core of anti-Semitism." One Treasury Department official referred to "swarms of Jews and a good many white men" engaging in illegal trade with the Confederacy. A newspaper correspondent described them as "pork-hating descendants of Abraham" and the "oleaginous children of Israel."[35] General Ulysses S. Grant, bedeviled by these speculators, placed the blame on Jewish merchants. In July 1862, he telegraphed General J. T. Quimby to "examine the baggage of all speculators. . . . Jews should receive special attention." He subsequently instructed one of his officers to "refuse all permits to come south of Jackson; . . . the Israelites especially should be kept out," and another that "no Jews are to be permitted to travel on the Rail Road southward from any point. They may go north and be encouraged in it but they are such an intolerable nuisance that the department must be purged of them." To General William T. Sherman—whose anti-Semitism certainly needed no further encouragement—Grant wrote on 5 December 1862 that "in consequence of the total disregard and evasion of orders by the Jews my policy is to exclude them so far as practicable from the Department." A year later he ordered all Jews, "as a class," expelled from the Department of the Tennessee within twenty-four hours, without exception, and would permit no Jews to receive a pass "to visit headquarters for the purpose of making personal application" for a redress of grievances.[36]

Almost immediately, as word of the order became known, a number of Jews protested by letter and telegram, and Jewish delegations visited the capital to do the same.[37] Congressman Elihu B. Washburne wrote to Lincoln defending the order, calling it "the wisest order yet made." Washburne told Grant that "your order touching the Jews has kicked up quite a dust among the Israelites. They came here in crowds and gave an entirely false construction to the order. . . . All the democrats were fierce to censure your action."[38] An irate senator, Lazarus Powell of Kentucky, described how the Jews of Paducah, men, women, and children, were driven from their homes. Many of them "were known to be as highly honorable and loyal citizens." Powell supported a motion of censure for this "most atrocious and illegal order. It is inhuman and monstrous. It would be unworthy of the most despotic government in Europe."[39] But others defended Grant. And many newspapers printed anti-Semitic news accounts. The *Washington Chronicle* commented that Jews "have been notorious for their fondness for illegitimate . . . modes of making money. . . . The prejudice which exists in all communities against Jews is intensified in the army. . . . We do not believe there will be found a dozen men in the army who will not approve of [Grant's order]."[40]

Some years later, as president, Grant apologized to American Jews. "It never would have been issued," he explained, "if it had not been telegraphed the moment it was penned, and without reflection."[41] But at the time, Congress did nothing. As Republicans, a few years before, attempted to capitalize upon the Mortara case by criticizing the Buchanan administration, now Democrats tried to embarrass the Republican administration by asking that Grant be censured. But Lincoln had rescinded the order three weeks after it was issued (17 December 1862–7 January 1863). The motion to censure was tabled in the lower house fifty-six to fifty-three, and in the Senate, thirty to seven. General Henry Halleck explained to Grant that "the President has no objection to your expelling traitors and Jew peddlers, which, I suppose, was the object of your order; but, as it in terms proscribed an entire religious class, some of whom are fighting in our ranks, the President deemed it necessary to revoke it."[42]

Revoking an obviously anti-Semitic order was a matter of simple justice. Recognizing that the United States was a Christian country by amending the Constitution need not be construed as anti-Semitic, and the founders of the National Reform Association had reason to believe that Abraham Lincoln would support their cause. He was a religious man, his thoughts shaped by the Bible and the evangelical culture of the Illinois frontier. The fact that Lincoln did not belong to any church was, rather than being a disturbing characteristic, suited to the ecumenical nature of their task. Moreover, he had provided proof of his supreme Protestantism in a remarkable proclamation. The United States Senate, on 4 March 1863, unanimously passed a resolution, introduced by James Harlan of Iowa, calling upon the president to set apart a day of "prayer and humiliation." The resolution deplored "the national offenses which have provoked His righteous judgment" and used specific Christian phraseology in referring to "His appointed way through Jesus Christ."[43] There was neither debate nor discussion on the resolution. Lincoln's response, however, was all that the evangelists could have hoped. Previous presidents had issued similar proclamations during periods of emergency but had been careful to use abstract phrases, avoiding any Christian identifications. Lincoln did the opposite. His proclamation spoke of "our national sins," repeated that Americans "have forgotten God" in their pursuit of material prosperity, and—in an explicit and unprecedented statement—recognized "the sublime truth announced in the Holy Scriptures"; 30 April 1863 became National Fast Day.[44]

Thus the convention minutes of the early meetings of the National Reform Association were filled with a sense of fervor and optimism. Congress appeared to them to be sympathetic to their cause. Lincoln was a religious man, quintessentially Christian. Famous theologians trumpeted the idea. College presidents and professors, governors and former governors, state and federal judges of the highest rank, along with bishops, lawyers, public administrators, and important private citizens joined their ranks. The Reverend Charles S. Finney of Oberlin became an honorary vice-president. Senator B. Gratz Brown of Missouri wrote in support of the organization. William Strong, a Pennsylvania judge in 1863 who was shortly to become a Supreme Court justice, addressed the earliest meetings.[45] (He was later to serve as president of the National Reform Association.) "It can never be out of season to explain and enforce mortal dependence on Almighty God," Senator Charles Sumner wrote on 22 January 1864 to one of the founders, "or to declare the liberty and equal rights of all men—in other words, to assert the Fatherhood of God and the Brotherhood of man. Here are the two great commandments which no Christian can forget—in one the duty of grace and piety, and in the other the duty and grace of humanity."[46] The National Reform Association announced that "no practical opposition, either in public or private, had been made to the movement, and the moral portion of the community in the different States have on all occasions heartily endorsed it." All that was needed was "sufficient publicity" to achieve their object.[47]

The "practical opposition" came largely from Jews. Isaac Leeser warned his readers in 1863 not to take the National Reform Association lightly; that it was not the work of a single minor sect of Presbyterians but a powerful interdenominational Protestant combination; that its "poison has become more diffused . . . more portentous, and indicative of a coming storm"; that it threatened not only Jews, but Unitarians, deists, atheists, and Catholics as well; that Jews would have to join with Catholics to fight it.

> At present they would be as much injured as we, should the religious element be engrafted on the Constitution; for they would find it difficult to contend against a united Protestant body. We may therefore expect that should the question grow into larger dimensions, we should not be left alone to contend for human rights, but find support no less from our ancient oppressors than from persons indifferent to all religion, not from love of Israelites and those who would be excluded under the new state of things, but from a sense of common danger.[48]

Initially a few Jewish leaders advised against taking any action, because "agitating the question might perchance lend it too much importance, while silence would be the best means of defeating it."[49] Such a course was soon abandoned. Jews carefully monitored National Reform Association tactics, responding to each one with appropriate measures. When Cincinnati Presbyterians endorsed the National Reform Association platform by petitioning Congress on 20 September 1864 that a "Christian nation with an atheistical Constitution is an anomaly," and that "*now* is the time to make this correction of fundamental error when God is baptizing the nation in blood, in order, as we trust, to purify it from destructive evils, so as to preserve our nationality and give us in the end peace and prosperity," the Board of Delegates of American Israelites countered it, arguing "that this omission of a creed has not been hurtful to Christianity any more than to Judaism. . . . Your memorialists cannot believe that the land is cursed by God, because He has not been recognized in the Constitution, or else, they would respectfully ask, why have eighty years of prosperity blessed it on land and sea, in its basket and kneading trough, in field and city." [50]

Myer Isaacs, secretary of the Board of Delegates of American Israelites, had interviews with Senators Charles Sumner and Lyman Trumbull (chairman of the judiciary committee) and "received their assurance that the object of the Philadelphia convention [of the National Reform Association] did not have their sympathy. . . . If, however, the question should come before the Senate in definite shape, the Board of Delegates should be at once afforded an opportunity of appearing in opposition." [51] In fact, Senator Sumner withdrew his support for the Christian amendment as quickly as it had been offered. When some of his "Hebrew friends" in Massachusetts indicated their dissatisfaction with his endorsement, Sumner expressed his "astonishment at what you say of my favoring any proposition to disfranchise anybody. It is all an invention or misapprehension. I have said that I should not object to a recognition of God by formal words in the Constitution—thus, for instance, saying, 'We the people of the United States, acknowledging God as the ruler of nations,' etc. This is all; I take it no Hebrew would differ with me on this point." [52]

Other public figures failed to respond to National Reform Association overtures. The association appointed committees to publicize its activities in different cities and sections of the country. In Hartford, Connecticut, it believed the best person to head such a committee was Dr. Horace Bushnell, and so informed him. [53] But Bushnell never acknowledged this nomination, never corresponded with the National Reform Association, never endorsed its program. Obviously he disagreed with it.

The same may be said for Lincoln. Jews never lost their faith that Lincoln would resist the proposed Christian amendment, despite his failure to reprimand Grant, his Sunday order to military commanders, and his National Fast Day proclamation. Their faith was merited. Lincoln's Fast Day proclamation had been a true expression of his religious beliefs, but thereafter he chose his public words with greater care. It is probable that Lincoln realized that the proclamation had helped spur a movement that was dangerous to religious liberty. On 10 February 1864 a large delegation of National Reform Association members called upon Lincoln and read to him their resolutions, an address, and a memorial to Congress containing their proposed constitutional amendment. One of the resolutions singled out Lincoln's Fast Day proclamation as "pleasing evidence that God is graciously inclining the hearts of those who are in authority over us to recognize His hand in the affairs of the nation." Their address to Lincoln made the same point.

> We are encouraged, Mr. President, to hope that you will give the great object for which we pray, your cordial and powerful support, because you have already shown by many significant acts of your administration that the principle on which it rests is dear to your heart. . . . You, moreover, as no other of our Chief Magistrates ever did, have solemnly reminded us of the redeeming grace of our blessed Savior, and of the authority of the Holy Scriptures over us as a people. By such acts as these you have awakened a hope in the Christian people of this land that you represent them in feeling the want of a distinct and plain recognition of the divine authority in the Constitution of the United States.[54]

Lincoln heard them out and responded in the time-honored manner of a politician, with caution: "Gentlemen: The general aspect of your movement I cordially approve. In regard to particulars I must ask time to deliberate, as the work of amending the Constitution should not be done hastily. I will carefully examine your paper in order more fully to comprehend its contents than is possible from merely hearing it read, and will take such action upon it as my responsibility to my Maker and our country demands."[55] In the remaining fourteen months of his life Lincoln took no action endorsing or supporting the National Reform Association.

Nor did Congress, which tabled the memorial of the National Reform Association as well as all subsequent petitions of a similar nature. Scarcely a year passed without a number of these petitions being submitted, for the National Reform Association continued to be quite active. One can measure the decline of its influence by the degree of concern voiced in the annual reports of the Board of Delegates of American Israelites. In 1866 the executive committee of the Board of Delegates congratulated itself on its "timely efforts" and the "liberal and statesmanlike views of the Senate" in defeating the efforts of the National Reform Association but concluded that "it is not impossible, in view of . . . the persistency with which they harass Congress and the people, that a more powerful movement of a similar character may yet be initiated. In such a contingency we must be well prepared to meet the advancements of sectarianism by firm, resolute action."[56] By 1868 the executive committee reported with confidence that "there is little immediate likelihood of such a sectarian measure receiving the sanction of public opinion. The committee would nevertheless recommend that the subject be kept in mind."[57]

Congress was well satisfied with and had no intention of altering the religious provisions of the Constitution. In February 1869, at the same time that an Illinois petition was presented "praying for an amendment to the Constitution of the United States, recognizing the obligations of the Christian religion," Congress was deep in debate on the proposed Fifteenth Amendment. Senator Henry Wilson wished its wording enlarged so that no state could deprive a citizen of the franchise or the right to hold office, "on account of race, color, nativity, property, education, or religion." The constitution of one state, New Hampshire, still excluded non-Protestants from state office. Senator Oliver P. Morton argued that the "exclusion is contrary to the whole spirit of our institutions. . . . Are we at liberty to reject [Wilson's proposal] and thus to say to New Hampshire, in substance and by implication, that she may continue to exclude men from office on account of their faith?" Senator John Sherman agreed with both of his colleagues. "It is wise," he stated, "to wipe out a multitude of discriminations in the constitutions of the several states." Senator James H. Patterson of New Hampshire explained that the exclusion was a "dead letter," that Catholics held seats in the legislature, and that "the people of the State would not object to having that restriction in our constitution set aside." (In 1876 that discriminatory provision finally was removed, as we have noted, but by only a narrow margin.) While Congress debated the limits of the Fifteenth Amendment, the tenor of its remarks was to preserve the separation of church and state nationally. Not a single member spoke in behalf of the Illinois petition.[58]

During this period the figure of greatest national prominence to endorse the program of the National Reform Association was Supreme Court Justice William Strong. When President Grant nominated him for the court in 1870, a group of Jews protested the appointment. The journal of the National Reform Association, *The Christian Statesman*, proudly reported the way in which Strong responded.

> It was known privately that the Jews and others in eastern cities had circulated petitions against his confirmation because he had publicly approved the Christian Amendment to the Constitution. A deputation of the Jews in Philadelphia waited upon him with the frank statement that they would oppose his confirmation to the extent of their influence. Judge Strong met them with the simple answer that he did not propose in any way to interfere with them because of their faith; but they did now propose to employ their influence to exclude from the service of the nation, not only himself, but on the same ground, every other man who believed and avowed his faith in Jesus Christ as the Ruler of nations. He submitted that not he but they were open to the charge of intolerance. One of them discerned his point and frankly admitted they had made a mistake in coming there; others, however, still insisted that it was a matter of vital importance with them, and that they would not withdraw their opposition.[59]

Strong remained president of the National Reform Association from 1867 to 1873, when he was replaced by Felix R. Brunot, chairman of the Board of Indian Commissioners. By then, instead of being an ecumenical movement, the association had narrowed to a membership of fundamentalist Presbyterians and Methodists; and instead of being a national movement, it drew its main support from the small towns and rural regions of the Midwest.[60] Jews no longer stood alone in sounding the alarm against the Christian amendment. The Seventh-Day Adventists, for example, considered the National Reform Association "a powerful organization" that threatened religious freedom. "Slowly, but steadily, the friends of this movement are bringing it to the public notice and enlarging the circle of its active supporters," warned one

Adventist. "They have convinced themselves that they are called by God to a mighty work. They believe they have a noble mission."[61] But *The Independent* in New York City dismissed the National Reform Association as a group of deluded fanatics. "We cannot resist the conviction that its advocates are engaged in the most hopeless of all undertakings. . . . Nothing short of a largely predominant public sentiment could secure the [passage of a Christian amendment]. No such sentiment now exists, and there is not the remotest possibility of creating it by any amount of discussion."[62] The New York *Herald* reported upon the national convention of the National Reform Association in 1873 with a scathing account: "Scattered throughout the house [Cooper Institute] might be seen a surprising number of white-crowned and venerable heads, whose snowy coronals lent to the sober body an air of great sagacity and dignity—appearances which are not of small value, because of the impression which they commonly produce upon unsophisticated minds." The headline of the account read: "GOD AND GOVERNMENT / PIOUS PALAVERING / THE NOBLE FRAMERS OF THE REPUBLIC CRITICIZED AND DISSECTED / HISSES AND PLAUDITS. The following day the headline read: TALK AND TRAVAIL / MUCH ADO WITH NOTHING DONE / ONSLAUGHT OF AN ORATOR UPON JEWS, JESUITS, INFIDELS, ATHEISTS, AND PAGANS ALIKE. These news accounts had been preceded by a slashing editorial in the *Herald*: "However we may acquit the projectors of the amendment of an intentional irreverence on account of purblindness, we do not hold them guiltless of a deliberate intention to abridge the liberty of conscience in America. Their pretensions once acknowledged, a Jew or an infidel would be outside the constitution. By this means the first limitation of conscience would be achieved. The elimination of objectionables would pave the way for further aggressions, and the first steps would be taken to the formation of a State Church. Herein lies the magnitude of the danger from permitting meddling with the constitution."[63] On the other hand, a New York City Methodist newspaper, *Christian Advocate*, gave full support to the National Reform Association. "The fundamental proposition on which this whole movement is based," commented the editors, "is the impossibility of State neutrality in religion and morals. Once grant this fundamental principle, and we see not how the object of this movement can be logically opposed or ignored."[64]

Yet the National Reform Association persevered. Its organ, *The*

Christian Statesman, appeared regularly as a monthly publication. In the closing decades of the nineteenth century, as its goal became less attainable, as its number dwindled, the fanaticism of the remnant of the association became more apparent. Still, it could usually muster a few retired politicians who had nothing to lose to speak in favor of the amendment. Robert Furnas, ex-governor of Nebraska, and Roswell Farnham, ex-governor of Vermont, did so, thus helping to preserve an air of legitimacy to the organization. More important, a number of judges publicly supported its aims, including Supreme Court Justice David J. Brewer, who was reported to be "an ardent lecturer for the National Reform Association."[65] The association continued to petition Congress. It held conferences and conventions, sponsored summer camps, supported speakers, cooperated with prohibitionists, launched anti-Mormon crusades, yet it neither forsook nor compromised its goal to put Christ into the Constitution. When Congressman Morris Sheppard of Texas introduced a bill in 1910 to change the preamble of the Constitution to read, "In the name of God . . . ," the National Reform Association rejected the proposal as inadequate. "This no more ties up the government to Christian ethics," commented *The Christian Statesman*, "than it does to the ethics of Mormonism and Islam."[66]

In a sense the membership of the National Reform Association lived on history, recalling it and twisting it to serve their needs. Constantly they harked back to the Civil War. Jesus Christ had given victory to the North. He had called into existence the National Reform Association for an exalted purpose: to correct a defect in the fundamental law. In 1895 an author pointed out what he considered to be a fallacy in National Reform Association logic.

> It may be remarked in passing that the force of the argument in favor of the amendment which was drawn from the Civil War, regarded as a punishment inflicted upon the nation for the dishonoring of God in its organic law, has been greatly weakened by the fact that blessings of incalculable value have resulted from the war: the extinction of slavery, and the industrial regeneration of the Southern States. The war may have been a divine infliction upon the nation for its sins, but surely it could not have been for this sin of omission, for the blessings resulting from the war have been accumulating, while the alleged sin has been persisted in.[67]

But no contrary argument could shake the membership's belief that the National Reform Association was divinely inspired. The origin of their movement, one member wrote in 1912, occurred "during the darkest days of the civil war, when men's hearts were failing them for fear, and when they instinctively turned to the God of nations for deliverance."[68] In those dark days of fratricidal conflict, wrote another member in 1933, on the seventieth anniversary of the founding of the National Reform Association, "men of vision, deep thought, and prayer, sensed that there was something wrong in our national life. We must have grievously sinned against God since He seemed to have turned a deaf ear to our prayers." Abraham Lincoln's proclamation of National Fast Day was heard by the Lord:

> On the following Saturday General Stonewall Jackson was fatally wounded, by accident. Stonewall Jackson was the brains of the Southern Army. He was known to be a good Christian man but he was an obstructionist. God removed the obstruction by taking General Jackson to Heaven. After this day of national humiliation, confession, and prayer the tide turned; the North won one battle after another until at last victory perched upon our banners.[69]

Thus, the National Reform Association labored with extraordinary tenacity through wars and depressions, promising to "save the nation" if only the people would heed its call to put Christ into the Constitution. In 1945 the organization finally dissolved, but the National Association of Evangelicals then took up the cause, endorsing a Christian amendment by which "this nation devoutly recognizes the authority and law of Jesus Christ, Savior and Ruler of nations, through whom are bestowed the blessings of Almighty God."[70] It was an old cause, as old as the nation. Its peak came during a period of war, a time of enormous psychological stress, when moderate Protestants, without much reflection regarding the political consequences and constitutional ramifications, supported the movement. The United States brushed the possibility of becoming a Christian state by the fundamental law of the land. With peace, the danger receded, and Americans consistently rejected appeals of the National Reform Association, agreeing with Horace Greeley's dictum: "The name of God on a plow beam would not make the plow run any better."[71]

We Are Yet Strangers in Stranger Lands

The tide of Protestantism rose markedly in the middle third of the nineteenth century. Their organizations proliferated. Their proselytizing activities were well financed and began to extend beyond America to the Far East. As early as 1816 Thomas Jefferson commented that Protestant Bible societies, "finding that the days of fire and faggot are over in the Atlantic hemisphere, are now preparing to put the torch to the Asiatic regions." [1] *Their goal was to make the nation distinctively Christian legally and to use the American flag to further their mission of converting the world. In 1832 the Episcopal bishops of America affirmed the presumption that "the Christian religion [is] part of the law of the land." So did a book published in 1828,* An Inquiry into the Moral and Religious Character of the American Government, *which was ascribed to the pen of Senator Theodore Frelinghuysen of New Jersey: "Is liberty of conscience to be confounded with the license that acts against conscience? . . . Are christian institutions to be administered by unchristian agents?" Professor Taylor Lewis, in an article entitled "Has the State a Religion?" in the* American Whig Review, *maintained that "religion—revealed religion, Christianity—should regulate legislation."* [2] *Bela Bates Edwards, editor of a Protestant religious journal, wrote: "Perfect religious liberty does not imply that the govern-*

> *ment of a country is not a Christian government. . . .*
> *Most, if not all, of our constitutions of government*
> *proceed on the basis of the truth of the Christian*
> *religion."* [3]
>
> *The constitutional impact of this aggressive Prot-*
> *estantism can be measured by comparing the Ameri-*
> *can treaty with Tripoli with two others (China and*
> *Switzerland), which were signed more than half a*
> *century later.*

Treaty with Tripoli

During the depression of 1929 the minuscule remnant of the National Reform Association must have been immensely pleased to read in *The Christian Statesman* an exposé regarding an old treaty under the headline "Tripoli Treaty Fraud Uncovered." Ratified by the United States in 1797, one provision, Article 11, particularly galled the association's membership. Article 11 read:

> As the government of the United States of America *is not in*
> *any sense founded on the Christian religion*—as it has in itself
> no character of enmity against the laws, religion or tranquility of
> Musselmen—and as the said States never have entered into any
> war or act of hostility against any Mehomitan nation, it is de-
> clared by the parties that no pretext arising from religious opin-
> ions shall ever produce an interruption of the harmony existing
> between the two countries. [4]

The initial words of Article 11 had been cited hundreds of times in numerous court cases and in political debates whenever the issue of church-state relations arose. On one side of the debate were those who used the words of the treaty to strengthen their position that the Constitution mandated a complete equality for all religions, which meant a recognition of and favoritism towards none. As late as 1911 the Religious Liberty Association reprinted a study edited by William A. Blakely of the University of Chicago, which contained his comment that Article 11 "is simply a plain and unequivocal statement, though negative in form, of the absolute equality, as far as our government is concerned, of other religions with the Christian religion."[5] Jews frequently referred to the article in discussions of a much-debated question, whether or not the United States was a Christian nation. Fundamentalist Protestants, on the other hand, argued that the founding fathers were Christian, that they never "officially denied the Christian character of our nation," and that Christianity was part of our common law and entitled to legal and constitutional preference. As Richard C. Wylie of the National Reform Association put it in 1905, "Our free government would be impossible without our Christian civilization; our civilization is produced and perpetuated by the Christian religion."[6] That logic attracted many Protestants who could not be classified as fundamentalists. They dismissed the Tripoli treaty as an aberration. In one instance an angry judge of the Minnesota Supreme Court attacked Article 11, claiming that "a fugitive expression in an obscure treaty . . . is a poor foundation upon which to rest a constitutional principle."[7]

The "fraud" reported by *The Christian Statesman* dealt with the findings of Dr. C. Snouk Hurgronje, who in 1930 published the results of his examination of the treaty documents, which revealed that Article 11 of the English translation had no meaningful equivalent in the original Arabic. Article 11 in the Arabic text, he noted, consisted of "a letter from Hassan Pasha of Algiers to Yussuf Pasha of Tripoli. . . . Three quarters of the letter consists of an introduction, drawn up by a stupid secretary who just knew a certain number of bombastic words and expressions in solemn documents."[8] Obviously someone added the English words, and the most likely suspect is Joel Barlow, who as counsel to Algiers was responsible for effecting the treaty. Barlow had been born and reared in conservative Connecticut and had served as a Congregational chaplain in the revolutionary army. But after his residence in Europe, beginning in 1788, and his association with Girondist leaders, he abandoned Christian orthodoxy for Enlightenment rationalism. "The Puritan lad, with generations of Puritan blood in his veins, nurtured at Yale College—then the cradle of Federalism—bursts his chrysalis," wrote his biographer, "and appears in religion a liberal, in politics a pronounced Republican." (John Adams had once commented that even Thomas Paine was "not a more worthless fellow" than Joel Barlow.) That Barlow wished to clarify the non-Christian nature of the American republic was evident in his *Advice to the Privileged Orders*, penned five years before the Tripoli treaty.

> In the United States of America there is, strictly speaking, no such thing as a church, and yet in no country are the people more religious. All sorts of religious opinions are entertained there, and yet no heresy among them at all. All modes of worship are practised, and yet there is no schism. Men frequently change their creed and their worship, and yet there is no apostasy. They have ministers of religion, but no priests. In short, religion is there a personal and not a corporate concern.[9]

Perhaps the most extraordinary use of Article 11 occurred in 1899, when a United States diplomat (who was Jewish) had it translated into Turkish and presented to the sultan in Constantinople in order to save American lives in the Philippines. Oscar S. Straus in his recollections, *Under Four Administrations*, does not say how he knew about Article 11—he might well have seen it cited in a Jewish periodical—merely that it was "pertinent information . . . as to our Government's attitude." (Sunnite Mohammedans who resided in the Philippines recognized the sultan of Turkey as their spiritual head. They had always resisted Spanish rule, and the United States, now in military possession of those islands, hoped that the sultan would use his influence with them to accept American authority.) Straus recalls that when the sultan read Article 11 "his face lighted up," and he agreed to telegraph Sunnite chiefs there to cooperate with the Americans. The tactic worked. Mohammedans in the Philippines refused to join Emilio Aguinaldo's insurrectionary forces.[10]

Some other twentieth-century uses of Article 11 have been trivial, if not ridiculous. For example, in 1955 the American Association for the Advancement of Atheism declared that George Washington was its author. A California congressman, Edgar W. Heistand, denounced this "most flagrant misquotation for evil purposes," explaining that Article 11 derived from "the imagination of the translator, a latter day bureaucrat named Joel Barlow."[11]

What is significant about the Tripoli treaty was not Barlow's deception, however, but its ready acceptance by the government. Not a word of protest was raised against Article 11 in 1797. Secretary of State Timothy Pickering endorsed and John Adams transmitted the treaty to the Senate with a customary message. Federalists and Republicans in the Senate approved it without objection. Whatever their personal feelings on the question of religious equality for non-Christians in particular states, all concurred that Article 11 comported with the principles of the Constitution. Furthermore, two decades later, when the first diplomatic appointment of a Jew—Mordecai M. Noah as consul to Tunis—was terminated on the grounds of religion, the Tripoli treaty was cited by Noah as corroboration of the constitutional intent "that the religion of a citizen is not a legitimate object of official notice from the government." Madison, Jefferson, and John Adams, in private letters to Noah, expressed their agreement.[12]

Treaty with China

Yet Jews, a half century later, chose to ignore the significance of Article 29 of the China treaty (1858), despite the efforts of Isaac Leeser to arouse their interest. Leeser saw plainly that Protestant forces were breaching the wall of separation between church and state to serve their own interests. Unlike Article 11 of the Tripoli treaty, which was declarative in intent, Article 29 of the China treaty was substantive and of benefit to Christians only; it was written by an unordained Protestant minister; and it was ratified by the Senate almost unanimously. Most ominous of all, no one in the government appeared to be troubled by its violation of constitutional principle. Article 29 stipulated:

> The principles of the Christian religion as professed by the Protestant and Roman Catholic churches, are recognized as teaching men to do good; and to do to others as they would have others do to them. Hereafter, those who quietly profess and teach these doctrines shall not be harassed or persecuted on account of their faith. Any person, whether citizen of the United States or Chinese convert, who according to these tenets peaceably teach and practise the principles of Christianity, shall in no case be interferred with or molested.[13]

Thus by a treaty, part of the supreme law of the land, the United States government provided for the protection of American Christians and their converts in China. Not for a moment did its author, S. Wells Williams, who served as secretary and interpreter at the American embassy, consider that such an article contradicted the Constitution. Nor did it cross the mind of William B. Reed, the American diplomat in charge of the negotiations, who permitted Williams a free hand in dealing with Chinese authorities on this subject.[14] The only member of the Senate to vote against the treaty, Jefferson Davis of Mississippi, did so without explanation.[15] There was scarcely any protest from the public, or in the press, or from liberal pulpits. Isaac Leeser was the exception. Disturbed by the lack of reaction, he wrote in *The Occident*:

> It is, indeed, a misfortune, that the government of the United States has been so unlucky or imprudent as to entrust the making of treaties to sectarians, who look upon *their own associates as constituting the whole people of the Union*. . . . The attempts now so abundantly made to engraft a Christian or sectarian coloring on the laws, are utterly subversive of the glorious work which was accomplished in 1788. . . . There can be no doubt but that the far greater number of Americans are oftener Christians in name than from a sincere belief in the dogmas which are the foundation of their professed faith. We have a right, therefore, to complain of that coward deference to a supposed public opinion, which yields to what it believes to be its interest, and would surely not do so, were it convinced how many there are who agree with it in opinion on matters of religion. . . . And still, while indifference is so rampant, every politician tries to show *his* particular devotion to the cause of Christianity, in order, no doubt, to gain the public applause. . . . It were to be wished that men of better common sense, of more honesty, and more consideration of the fundamental law of the land were in future to be entrusted with the making of treaties, especially with semi-civilized nations.[16]

Leeser might have been describing William B. Reed, who had no real interest in Article 29 and at one stage was prepared to sign a treaty without any mention of religion. "Now, gentlemen," Reed told Williams and his missionary associate, William Martin, "if you can get your article in—all right! But, with or without it, I intend to sign on the 18th of June." Martin thought Reed vain and offensive, a person of "no fixed principles," who approved of Article 29 "in hopes of currying favor with religious communities at home. He said to us (Dr. Williams and myself) in so many words—words that we felt as an insult— that he expected us to make the religious people of our country fully sensible of what he had done for their cause."[17]

Williams and Martin, of course, were overjoyed on several counts. Catholics had a long head start in the race for Chinese converts. Only a dozen years earlier a high Chinese official commented, "Originally I did not know that there were these differences in their [Christian] religious practises." [18] A distinguishing Chinese language character was devised to differentiate between Catholics and Protestants. Their missionaries were accorded equal treatment (and considerable mistreatment) and were restricted to particular geographic areas. The treaty of 1858 is important because what had been granted previously by the whim of Chinese officials was now solemnized by a sovereign agreement that clearly specified the protection of Protestants as well as Catholics; moreover, it removed the geographic limits of their activities. "Before 1858," Tyler Dennett noted in his study, *Americans in Eastern Asia*, "the missionary suffered far more from the restriction imposed upon him than did the merchant. Consequently the missionary was the more impatient for greater liberty under treaty protection." [19]

In Tientsin, Williams addressed a meeting of Protestant missionaries gathered to celebrate Article 29. He told them that their task would be hard, that "laws and treaties do not restrain the wicked heart of men," but that the way was now open. The British, impressed by the American example, also insisted upon a similar provision in their treaty with China. There was a good deal of cooperation between the Protestant missionaries of both nations. In his private journal, Williams, a rabid anti-Catholic, exulted that Article 29, and Article 8 of the British treaty, will "prove a great boon to the Chinese Christians when, as I fear it will, Romanism becomes powerful and uses its power to oppress and reduce the people of the land who may refuse to join that form." [20]

There were remnants of Jews in China, the descendants of the introduction of that religion almost a thousand years earlier. Two Chinese converts to Protestantism visited one such colony at Kaifeng in 1850 at the request of the London Society for Promoting Christianity among the Jews. [21] The Reverend William Martin revisited that colony in 1866, remarking upon their sorry state: Their synagogue was wrecked, and the meaning of their rituals was all but forgotten. Some, he noted, obviously unaware of his anti-Semitic slur, remained "true to their hereditary instincts" by engaging in money lending. "I endeavored to comfort them by pointing to Him who is the consolation of Israel," he recalled. Martin also wrote to a Jewish newspaper in New York City proposing the formation of a Jewish mission.[22] None was ever sent. Some years earlier Isaac Leeser had tried to drum up Jewish interest in a "proposed mission to China." Our "brethren [in China] are threatened with extermination by the meddling missionaries of various denominations," Leeser wrote in one essay. But in another he confessed being "ashamed to speak on this subject again, owing to the apathy existing, both here and in England, regarding the fate of so many Israelites [in China]."[23]

What most concerned Leeser was the necessity of maintaining a strict adherence to constitutional principles. "Little *practical* injury will result" from the 1858 treaty with China, Isaac Leeser conceded, but even "a *theoretical* wrong is an infringement on our rights, and ought to be resisted *in limine*. Vigilance is the price of justice."[24] Thereafter, Protestant missionary activity in the far East increased dramatically. Successive administrations clearly furthered its extension. "Humanity indeed demands and expects a continually extending sway of the Christian religion," Secretary of State William H. Seward wrote in 1867.[25] But subsequent treaties did avoid any recognition of special Christian prerogatives, and American Jews voiced no objections.

Treaty with Switzerland

Jewish concern that their constitutional rights be protected in treaties proved a difficult problem for the American government. To what extent it would insist upon those rights—that is, the equal treatment of its citizens abroad—was apparent in our diplomatic negotiations with Switzerland. Most Americans were not aware that some of the cantons in Switzerland had local laws that discriminated against Jews. In fact, they lauded Switzerland as a miniature version of the United States, a federal republic of free institutions. When President Zachary Taylor appointed Ambrose Dudley Mann as special agent to the Swiss Confederation in 1850, secretary of state John M. Clayton wrote instructions that complimented the Swiss on "the orderly deportment and character of its citizens. . . . At this period when the reactionary movement of continental Europe seems to threaten the obliteration of liberal political institutions we owe it to the character of our own free government, as well as to the commercial interests of our country to strengthen, by all the means at our disposal, the ties, which bind us to the Swiss Confederation, which like our own happy land is the home of the free."[26]

Mann signed a commercial treaty at Berne on 25 November 1850, the first article of which included the statement: "On account of the tenor of the Federal Constitution of Switzerland, Christians alone are entitled to the enjoyment of the privileges guaranteed by the present Article in the Swiss Cantons. But said cantons are not prohibited from extending the same privileges to citizens of the United States of other religious persuasions." Mann explained to Clayton's successor, Secretary of State Daniel Webster, that it would be an easy matter to convince individual cantons with restrictive laws to make exceptions for non-Christian citizens of the United States. The "privilege I am assured will never be denied," he wrote, to any Israelite "hailing from the United States." He reminded Webster that "it was more than thirty years, if I rightly remember, after the adoption of our constitution, before the Israelites were fully affranchised in Maryland."[27]

Webster saw "nothing to object to" in any part of the treaty. Nor did Taylor's successor, President Millard Fillmore, at least as far as the religious question was concerned. But American Jews did, and they were quick to voice their complaints.[28] Henry Clay presented to the Senate the memorial of "M. M. Noah and others, Israelites of New York, praying that certain provisions [in the treaty] interfering with their religious rights, be rejected." Clay wrote that he disapproved entirely of the restriction "under the operations of which a respectable portion of our fellow-citizens would be excluded from . . . benefits." Webster, responding to the complaints of Jacob Cardozo of South Carolina, noted that the defects of the article "concerning the Israelites have not escaped the attention of this Department, and . . . will be laid before the Senate."[29] Isaac Leeser also wrote to a number of senators, receiving answers from two (James Pearce of Maryland and John Berrien of Georgia) who assured him of their hostility "to the ratification of the provision which excludes Jews from equal rights." Leeser blessed the Senate for "watching over the constitutional guarantees" and publicly thanked Pearce and Berrien in *The Occident* "for the kind promptness with which they replied to our notes." (He also excoriated Mann for being "so ignorant of this country's institutions" and "hoped that the gentleman in question may have leave to spend the remainder of his days in retirement from public service.")[30]

Thus alerted, the Fillmore administration responded in positive and unqualified terms: The article was not acceptable. Fillmore's message to the Senate read:

> It is quite certain that neither by law, nor by treaty, nor by any other official proceeding is it competent for the Government of the United States to establish any distinction between its citizens founded on differences in religious beliefs. Any benefit or privilege conferred by law or treaty on one must be common to all, and we are not at liberty, on a question of such vital interest and plain constitutional duty, to consider whether the particular case is one in which substantial inconvenience or injustice might ensue. It is enough that an inequality would be sanctioned hostile to the institutions of the United States and inconsistent with the Constitution and the laws.
>
> Nor can the Government of the United States rely on the individual Cantons of Switzerland for extending the same privileges to other citizens of the United States as this article extends to Christians. It is indispensable not only that every privilege granted to any of the citizens of the United States should be granted to all, but also that the grant of such privilege should stand upon the same stipulation and assurance by the whole Swiss Confederation as those of other articles of the convention.[31]

On 7 March 1851, the Senate, by a vote of thirty-four to three, accepted the Swiss treaty with amendments, one of which was to strike the offensive words in the first article.

Despite this action, and the clarity of Fillmore's message, Mann accepted a rewording of the article, dictated by the Swiss, which did not alter its meaning. The substance was the same: "The citizens of the United States of America and the citizens of Switzerland, shall be admitted and treated upon a footing of reciprocal equality in the two countries, *where such admission and treatment shall not conflict with the constitutional or legal provisions, as well Federal as State and Cantonal of the contracting parties.*"[32] Mann believed it was the best that could be done. The Swiss could not constitutionally dictate to the cantons any more than the United States government could dictate to the states on questions of local jurisdiction.

The initial version was really more honest. It recognized that "Christians alone are entitled to . . . privileges" in many cantons. The second was a subterfuge. It provided for "reciprocal equality" but only where that equality did not conflict with cantonal law. In fact, the Swiss spelled this out in a note to Mann on 5 July 1852. The new wording, the note explained, "may cause uncertainty regarding the sense and the meaning of the texts and thus lead to misunderstandings, even to controversies in the application of the treaty which it is very important to avoid for the faithful execution of all its articles." But the Swiss acknowledged that "the President and the Senate of the United States desire to avoid the *appearance* of being willing to sanction in a treaty provisions contrary to the Constitution of the Union of North America."[33] Two years after he rejected the initial version of the first article in strong terms, Fillmore endorsed the revisions, declaring that the "modifications . . . appear to me to proceed upon a reasonable principle of compromise."[34] The reworded article did not conflict with the Constitution. As Webster's son-in-law, Assistant Secretary of State John Appleton, later stated, "In its present form, although it may not remove some difficulties with reference to those who profess the Israeltish faith, yet I do not see that it [constitutionally] discriminates against this class of our citizens in any mode whatever."[35]

The amendments to the treaty experienced long delays in the Senate. Not until 29 May 1854 was a definitive vote taken. During this time examples of Swiss anti-Semitism were brought to public attention, especially a new law enacted by the canton of Basel, which declared that "no Jew, without exception," could engage in "commerce, trade, or any handicraft," and that any citizen "who admits a Jew into his house" in any capacity could be fined FR 300. The French government objected and in fact threatened to expel all Swiss citizens from France if this law was not rescinded. The canton of Basel refused. A group of prominent Jews in New York City formed a committee to circulate a petition, which was then presented to Congress by Senator Lewis Cass in April 1854. "Their brethren in faith and fellow-citizens," read the petition, "are often necessarily absent in foreign lands. . . . When so absent, they are in very many instances deprived of most of their civil and religious rights, while the citizens and subjects of the lands thus intolerant, enjoy, under our laws, equal privileges with our citizens."[36]

Even before the petition was drafted, the new American consul in Switzerland, Theodore Fay, informed the Department of State of a specific case, that of an American citizen, Mr. Gootman, who had twice received orders to leave the canton of Neufchatel because he was Jewish. Fay labored to reverse that decision and succeeded in getting the authorities to unofficially permit Gootman to remain there on a temporary basis.

The Richmond, Virginia, *Daily Dispatch* noted that the amended first article of the Swiss treaty "does not remove the injustice and illiberality of which the Jewish people complain." The newspaper cited France's protest by way of comparison and commented upon "the singular spectacle of a republican Senate of America on the point of accepting a treaty, by which it succumbs to an invasion of the rights of conscience so flagrant that it drew forth an emphatic and angry menace from Louis Napoleon! . . . No member of the United States Senate ought ever to be returned to that body, or to be permitted again to hold any official station, who is so thoroughly ignorant or regardless of the institutions of his country as to sustain by his vote the bigoted, intolerant, anti-constitutional, anti-republican provision contained in the first article of the proposed treaty with Switzerland." [37]

Leeser reprinted the entire account in *The Occident*, adding his comment that "two years ago . . . the Senate of the United States, to their honor be it said . . . refused to ratify that obnoxious clause." But Dudley Mann had "again yielded to the silly prejudices of the Cantons against the Jews. . . . It is to be hoped that such a monstrosity will not be permitted to become the supreme law of the land." Leeser felt certain that it would be defeated as Senator Lewis Cass "will do his duty to protect Jews in their equality of claim to be viewed as American citizens." [38]

The Jews looked to Cass because of the long and consistent record of his work in behalf of religious equality, and his personal friendship with a number of Jews. Jonas Phillips Levy, then a resident of the capital following a swashbuckling career in Latin America, named one of his sons after him. When Levy helped to organize a Hebrew congregation in Washington, it was Cass who secured the congressional legislation permitting its incorporation. In February 1854, Cass replied to a letter from Levy, assuring him that "I desire to procure those [equal] rights for a Catholic in a Protestant, and for a Protestant in a Catholic country, and for a Jew in all countries, and such are the views that I shall express, when I come to make my remarks upon the subject."[39]

Although Cass supported the Jewish demand for equality, the major catalyst for the defense of American rights abroad came from Protestants who suffered discrimination in Catholic countries. For some years Congress received petitions from various Protestant groups detailing their experiences and praying for relief. Because the United States offered religious liberty to all foreigners traveling or residing in this country, they argued, other nations should do the same for Americans abroad. The treatment should be exactly reciprocal. And our ministers should be instructed to secure those rights in all treaties. In 1852, in response to these petitions, Congressman John A. Wilcox of Mississippi introduced resolutions to that effect in the lower house. There were objections, however, that the resolutions constituted interference with an executive function. "We have no right to instruct our ministers abroad," said Alexander Stephens of Georgia. "We have no right to speak to them. This matter can only be in the form of a suggestion to the President." The resolutions were referred to a committee, which took no action.[40]

The following year, on 17 February 1853, Senator Joseph Underwood of Kentucky submitted a report to the upper house that included similar recommendations.

> *Resolved*, That it would be just and wise on the part of the Government of the United States in future treaties with foreign nations to secure, if practicable, to our citizens residing abroad the right of worshipping God freely and openly according to the dictates of their own consciences by providing that they shall not be disturbed, molested or annoyed in any manner on account of their religious belief, nor in the proper exercise of their peculiar religion, either within their own private houses or in churches, chapels, or other places appointed for public worship; and that they shall be at liberty to build and maintain places of worship in convenient situations interfering in no way with or respecting the religion and customs of the country in which they reside.
>
> *Resolved*, further, That it would be just and wise in our future treaties with foreign nations to secure to our citizens residing abroad the right to purchase and own burial places and to bury

any of our citizens dying abroad in such places with those religious ceremonies and observances deemed appropriate by the surviving relatives and friends of the deceased.[41]

Even before the Underwood report was submitted, Cass was widely recognized as the major spokesman for achieving its goals. Jews were only one, and not particularly an important one, of several religious groups that addressed their appeals to Cass. The Maryland Baptist Union Association of Baltimore, for example, sent him a petition referring to their ill treatment abroad. Cass recommended it to the appropriate committee with an eloquent speech on 3 January 1853. A few days later the New York *Times* reported a mass meeting in that city of citizens who were protesting the long sentence of imprisonment of two Tuscan peasants, Francisco and Rosa Madiai, for reading a Protestant Bible.[42] (Catholic authorities reported their crime was plotting against the state.) Resolutions called for their release and for their emigration to America. But others dealt with the rights of Americans abroad.

> *Resolved*, That this meeting firmly believes that it is the duty of the Government of the United States to protect all our citizens in their religious rights, whilst residing or sojourning in foreign lands; approves in the fullest manner of the noble attempt of a distinguished senator from Michigan (General Cass) to call the attention of the Government and the public to this important subject; and entertains the confident hope that this Government will speedily secure to its citizens, by the express stipulations of *international treaties*, the right to worship God according to the dictates of their conscience in every foreign land.[43]

Cass was a liberal Presbyterian who genuinely believed in religious equality. (He was strict only in the matter of Sabbath observance. On one occasion, during the debates on the Wilmot Proviso, when Congress wished to extend its late Saturday-night session into Sunday, he refused to participate and forced an adjournment.)[44] Cass thought Mormonism a disgrace to Christianity, but he also disliked Protestant nativists, rebuffing any linkage of his position with theirs. He appeared genuinely shocked at opposition to the Underwood resolutions. Some dissent was voiced within Congress. Senator George E. Badger of North Carolina, in the guise of a hypothetical question, raised the issue of states' rights. "Suppose," said Badger, "if, in the interior organization of this Government, there should be a state or States prohibiting religious toleration." What position would the United States "occupy with foreign Governments in asking from them what we have not the power to secure to their citizens at home?"[45] Cass responded that Badger "is supposing an impossible case."

The major attack came from Archbishop John Hughes, the leading Catholic prelate in the United States. In 1851, in a critical public letter addressed to Horace Greeley, he stated that the Pope, "whose subjects are entirely Catholic and united in belief," is not "bound to throw the [papal] states open for the preaching of every form of Protestantism and infidelity." He enlarged upon this theme in several letters in 1853 and 1854, rebutting and surrebutting Cass. The latter had invented a new religion, Hughes declared, the "American" religion, which he insists has a right to protection in all countries. "Wherever he appears in foreign lands, the sovereignty of the State, in regard to all questions appertaining to religion, must fall back the moment he proclaims himself an American. And it shall be understood that when he arrives on the shore of such country, with a full measure of American atmosphere, American sunbeams, and American religion according to Mr. Cass, . . . he shall have the right to say and do what he thinks proper, provided always it be according to the dictates of his conscience." Hughes pointed to numerous instances of intolerance in the United States, where a similar freedom was not permitted. All countries regulate "liberty of action according to conscience . . . to a certain extent, by the enactment of positive laws. In some countries the range is wider, in others more restricted; but it is limited in all, not even excepting the United States." Senator Cass was broaching "a new national policy," Hughes believed, based on a "confusion of ideas." If the United States was prepared to change the laws and constitutions of European states "by the power of armies and navies," that is "another matter"; to do it by diplomacy will simply expose America "to ridicule." In conclusion, while he deplored bigotry, Hughes upheld the sovereign right to restrict not conscience—which was "universal, indestructible, and inviolable"—but freedom of action.[46]

Two weeks before the Senate voted on the amendments to the Swiss treaty, Cass answered Hughes in a major address on behalf of the Underwood resolutions. He was careful to cite examples of intolerance in both Catholic and Protestant countries. Thus, said Cass, the government of Portugal in 1852 decreed that "the celebrating of public acts or worship, not that of the Catholic religion, should be punishable with imprisonment." Similarly, a Spanish law "prohibited any stranger, whether domiciliated or traveling in Spain, from professing any other religion than that of the Catholic Apostolic Church of Rome." Various Swedish laws prohibited foreigners from engaging in missionary activities: "Processions and ceremonies usual among foreign religions shall be forbidden," "persons converted from the religion of the State [Lutheran] shall be punished," et cetera. Cass refused to accept Hughes's distinction between freedom of conscience and freedom of action; insisted that the United States had the right to "procure for American citizens abroad immunity from local laws, so far as these interfere with the liberty of worshipping God"; and denied that he was introducing a new policy. Cass failed to mention the Swiss treaty but swore that he was not espousing any sectarian cause. "I earnestly advocate the proper action of the Government, not less in favor of our brethren of the Hebrew faith, than in favor of their Christian fellow-citizens. The descendant of the Patriarchs, and the believer in Jesus Christ, are entitled to the same protection. Jew or Gentile, all are equal in this land of law and liberty; and as the former suffers most from illiberal persecution, his case is entitled to the most commiseration, and sure am I that public sentiment would strongly reprove any attempt to create a distinction between them."[47]

On 13 April 1854, Cass wrote to Isaac Leeser, promising that the first article of the Swiss treaty "will never receive the sanction of this body [the Senate]."[48]

Yet it did, unanimously, on 29 May 1854. Cass was absent that day, but his presence probably would have made no difference. To Jews it appeared that when the Senate spoke of religious equality for Americans abroad they meant Protestant Americans. The fact that the Underwood resolutions later passed by a vote of twenty-six to eight was no consolation. The language, to be sure, was nonsectarian, but these resolutions were introduced at the request of Protestants and seemed to be for their sole benefit. The Swiss treaty and the Reed treaty with China a few years later were ample proof to Jews that this was so.

How could it be, Isaac Leeser asked, after the Senate was well informed by memorials and by letters of the restrictive cantonal laws, and the assurance of Lewis Cass that the first article would not be ratified, that it was? "It would appear," Leeser concluded,

> that we are too unimportant as a class to render it worth the while of the conservators of the liberty of the state to prevent *our* rights from being damaged, provided only those of the majority remain intact. In short, let men say what they will, let them ridicule us as they please, it is true and certain that we are in *Galuth*; we have our theoretical rights; but practically they are dependent on the will of those who have numbers on their side; and if we make all the noise in the world, and brag aloud after our heart's content, *we are yet strangers* in stranger lands.[49]

Leeser was happy to see the mounting number of Jewish congregations awaken at last to the danger of their constitutional rights being denied and expressing their indignation at the Swiss treaty. Ratification had the good effect of unifying Jews, and Leeser wished to see their activities continued. "But the very fact that senators could pass such a clause after the attention of the leading members (Cass, Mason, Butler and Pearce) had been drawn to it," wrote Leeser, "leaves very little room for hope." Isaac M. Wise, in the *Israelite*, advised Jews to "Agitate! Call meetings! Engage the Press in your favor!!!! Israelites, free men and citizens! Let not the disgrace of the treaty . . . remain upon the history of our country. Do not stand the insult heaped upon the Jewish citizens by unprincipled diplomatists."

In the following years Jewish congregations in Pittsburgh, Baltimore, Washington, Cleveland, Chicago, Saint Louis, New York, Nashville, Charleston, and other cities passed resolutions of protest. The Chicago resolution recognized the right of Switzerland, a sovereign nation, to exclude "whom she pleases from her territory." Moreover, the United States should not abandon the American principle of "non-intervention in the affairs of sovereign states" by forcing "her own liberal views on Switzerland." But, it concluded, "the United States should not make treaties with any Power by which her own citizens are voluntarily disfranchised; such proscriptive treaties had better remain unmade than stand as a stain on our statute books, being an injury to our citizens, a reproach to our freedom, and a convention with tyranny."[50] Jewish delegates from several states, meeting in Baltimore in October 1857, adopted a memorial addressed to President James Buchanan. (Senator Stephen A. Douglas of Illinois had advised Chicago Jews to do this.) Their memorial stated:

> It has been argued, that the commercial advantages this country derives from that treaty, would justify a slight sacrifice of principle; and while your memorialists are satisfied that such are not your Excellency's sentiments, they nevertheless respond, that if such were the policy of our government, Europe's despots would soon ask us mockingly: 'What is the price of all your liberties?' Pecuniary considerations should certainly, least of all, induce a departure from principle. . . . If it is against the *Cantonal* laws of Switzerland that those citizens of the United States, who are Israelites, come within the benefits of that treaty, then it is at least as clearly against the Constitutional laws of the United States, that those citizens be excluded, and yet both Cantonal and Constitutional law of the contracting governments are guarded against a conflict with the articles of convention. The whole subject seems thus reduced to the question: Which of the two governments shall yield and waive its equal right of construction?[51]

The large majority of the secular press expressed agreement with the Jewish position. A headline over an article in one Chicago paper announced: "Middle-Aged Bigotry—American Government Implicated." The *Louisville Journal* called the treaty "deeply disgraceful . . . unjust and proscriptive." The *Shelbyville Republican Banner* pointed out that by the treaty American atheists and infidels enjoyed rights denied to American Jews in Switzerland. The *Washington Star*, on the other hand, dissented: "This government had no authority whatever to demand of Switzerland in making the treaty to accord to any citizen of the United States privileges they would not enjoy under her laws were they citizens of Switzerland. Had it been insisted on we would have no treaty whatsoever with Switzerland." A few other papers, such as the *Dubuque Express* and the *Charleston Courier*, agreed editorially with the *Star*. The *Charleston Evening News* responded: "The point at issue is not whether this government was bound to demand of Switzerland such a treaty, but whether it was not bound to refuse to make a treaty with Switzerland or with any other country which recognized a religious distinction between one class of citizens and another."[52]

Jonas Levy in 1857 informed his coreligionists that the new secretary of state, Lewis Cass, was "our sincere friend, who I can vouch for"; that Cass would leave "no stone unturned to abrogate these articles in the treaty." President James Buchanan received a Jewish delegation and "unequivocally promised a speedy and energetic course of action." (Isaac Wise, one of the delegates, told his readers that Buchanan said, "Gentlemen, I have given you my word and I will do it.") The delegates were satisfied and advised American Jews "to abstain from further agitation on the subject." [53]

What Cass and Buchanan meant, however, is not that they would try to renegotiate what had been ratified, but that they would instruct the United States representative in Switzerland to try to remedy the legitimate grievances of American Jews by persuading the Swiss cantons to alter their laws. The result was a slow and painstaking diplomacy, with Jews exhibiting periodic bursts of impatience born of frustration. In 1859 Jonas Levy told Cass that the "public are much dissatisfied at his delay on that important subject." Cass replied that the Department of State was entirely satisfied with the work of the American minister in Switzerland. In 1859 and again in 1860, Clement Vallandigham of Ohio introduced resolutions in the lower house calling upon the president to submit any correspondence "relating to that clause of the treaty . . . which discriminates against the privileges of citizens of the United States holding to the Hebrew faith and worship, visiting or sojourning in Switzerland." Vallandigham promised "in the next Congress, to debate at length" the issues involved. [54] The Civil War intervened and the issues were never debated. Abraham Lincoln and his secretary of state, William H. Seward, adopted the same strategy on the Swiss treaty as their predecessors.

For more than a decade there appeared in the Jewish press numerous accounts of the laws and treatment of Jews in various Swiss cantons. Jews had larger worries during this period—the Mortara case, Grant's discriminatory order, the anti-Semitism of the war years, and the proposed Christian amendment to the Constitution—that pushed the Swiss treaty into the background. But the executive committee of the Board of Delegates of American Israelites always included in their annual reports a section on what progress was achieved in Switzerland. Jews appreciated that the task was difficult, because Switzerland resisted the combined pressures of the French, the British, and the Dutch. Even the Persians' request for a treaty that would have recognized religious equality for its Mohammedan citizens visiting Switzerland had been rejected. An American optician, Sigmund Mulhauser, applied for residence in Basel Ville to carry on business and had been refused on religious grounds. The canton of Thurgau did the same. A liberal Swiss newspaper commented that "the Thurgovian Christianity must be in a very tottering state to be frightened by a son of Abraham." [55] The canton of Schwyz boasted that it was not necessary to have written anti-Hebrew laws, and they had none; their fixed policy was to refuse the right of domicile to any Hebrew.

The persistent efforts of the American minister, Theodore Fay, more than any other factor, was responsible for the ultimate liberalization of Swiss laws concerning Jews. He gathered precise information on these laws from every canton, dividing them into "the liberally disposed," "the absolutely restrictive," and "the absolutely free." He then listed the reasons expressed for maintaining the laws, such as a justifiable Christian prejudice against Jews; the fear that the Jews of Alsace would inundate the country; the impropriety of foreign governments interfering in their internal affairs; and, from Argovy, the reasoning that "if America seeks the emancipation of Jews in Switzerland, Switzerland would have a right to demand the abolition of slavery in the United States." Fay answered each objection in detail, and his commentary, the "Israelite Note," was published by the Federal Council of Switzerland, translated into German and French, and reprinted and discussed in various newspapers. In 1860 Fay reported with pride that "there is a continued visible movement of public opinion in the right direction." [56] His successor, George G. Fogg, continued the work, and in time a large number of cantons repealed or modified their anti-Semitic laws. American Jews realized that without Fay's efforts this would not have been possible. Not until 1874, however, when a new Swiss constitution was adopted that established religious liberty and gave the federal government exclusive authority over aliens, was the matter totally resolved.

Equal Rights Abroad

In the last quarter of the nineteenth century American Jews had reason to be pleased with the efforts of their government to protect the rights of its Jewish citizens abroad. (In fact, the United States went further, protesting the ill treatment of Jews who were not

American citizens.) The experience of the Swiss treaty undoubtedly served to sensitize the government. The constitutional rights of Jews had been sacrificed on the grounds of commercial advantage and a diplomacy of noninterference with the internal laws of other nations. It was a policy that the United States did not repeat. From the 1870s on, time and again, American diplomats lectured officials in eastern European countries, especially those in Russia, on the meaning of the Constitution and why the United States could not and would not accept discriminatory laws against its Jewish citizens. In 1879 Congress condemned Russia for discriminating "against one T. Rosenstraus, a naturalized citizen of the United States, by prohibiting him from holding real estate, after his purchasing and paying for the same, because of his being an Israelite." A joint resolution of Congress declared that "the rights of the citizens of the United States should not be impaired, at home or abroad, because of religious beliefs; and that, if existing treaties between the United States and Russia be found, as is alleged, to discriminate in this or any other particular . . . the President be requested to take immediate action to have the treaties so amended as to remedy this grievance."[57] In 1892 Congressman James Dungan of Ohio introduced a resolution demanding that the United States "sever our diplomatic relations with the Russian Government, till such time as that Government shall cease discrimination against the Hebrews because of their religious faith."[58]

The problem with Russia festered for many years. In 1907, for example, the Department of State issued a warning notice that

> *Jews*, whether they were formerly Russian subjects or not, are not admitted to Russia unless they obtain special permission in advance from the Russian Government, and this Department will not issue passports to former Russian subjects or to Jews who intend going to Russian territory, unless it has assurance that the Russian government will consent to their admission.[59]

Louis Marshall and Edward Lauterbach wrote to Secretary of State Elihu Root that

> the meaning of this announcement cannot be misunderstood.. It segregates from the mass of American citizens those of the Jewish faith, whether naturalized or native-born, and withholds from them one of the privileges of citizenship if they harbor the inten-

tion of visiting Russia without having first secured the consent of the Russian Government. All other citizens, of whatever race or creed, are assured an unlimited passport, and are guaranteed the absolute protection of our flag. They encounter no discrimination at the hands of our Government. They are subjected to no humiliation. They are not compelled to submit to any inquisitorial intrusion into their private purposes; nor are they forced to conform to any religious test."

Root acquiesced immediately and ordered the notice reworded; when that was not satisfactory, he allowed Marshall and Lauterbach to edit it until it was.[60]

Yet, having won political equality in the states that had barred them from office; having triumphed over the attempt to amend the Constitution by incorporating in it a recognition of the divinity of Christ; having fought, successfully, to be accorded equal rights abroad; Jews at the turn of the century still wondered whether or not they were equals in a land of equality or strangers in a land of Christians. Jewish journals continued to ask, "Is Ours a Christian Government?" "Is the United States a Christian Nation?" "Is This a Christian Nation?"[61]

Christianity Is a Part of the Common Law

"I do not know if all Americans have faith in their religion—for who can read the secrets of the heart— but I am sure they think it necessary to the maintenance of republican institutions," Alexis de Tocqueville wrote during the Jacksonian era. "For the Americans the ideas of Christianity and liberty are so completely mingled that it is almost impossible to get them to conceive of the one without the other." [1] *Some fifty years later another foreign visitor, James Bryce, noted that "the National government and the State governments do give to Christianity a species of recognition inconsistent with the view that civil government should be absolutely neutral in religious matters." Bryce cited the opening of congressional and state legislative proceedings with prayers; Thanksgiving Day proclamations of a religious nature; Bible reading in public schools; laws punishing blasphemy against Christianity; and laws forbidding trade or labor on Sunday. He concluded, "The whole matter may, I think, be summed up by saying that Christianity is in fact understood to be, though not the legally established religion, yet the national religion."* [2]

Jews had no objection to legislative prayers if their rabbis were occasionally selected to offer them; or to mentions of God in official proclamations, so long as the divinity was not identified as Christian. Indeed, many Jews (though certainly not all) favored the exemption of church property from taxation and even supported the allocation of state funds to religious schools, so long as they received their share. Jews were quite willing to breach the separation of church and state if it was done nondenominationally. Although some Jews argued against state Sunday laws as an unconstitutional infringement of their religious freedom, others advocated removing the problem by switching their religious services from Saturday to Sunday.

Blasphemy

Jews did not go about "maliciously and openly" blaspheming Christianity, at least not since the Maryland case of Jacob Lumbrozo in the seventeenth century (the facts of which are few and questionable). It was difficult enough contending for equality without gratuitously offending a Christian population that harbored ambivalent feelings toward their Jewish fellow citizens. Besides, Jews wanted no association with those eccentrics and freethinkers who were charged with blasphemy in the nineteenth century. But Sunday laws—or Sabbath laws, or Lord's day laws, as they were called—had the same Christian ancestry and involved the same common-law assumptions as blasphemy. The two had a common stem. To a degree both called into question comparable constitutional issues. To punish one for blasphemy, it was maintained, limited the guarantees of free speech and free press; to punish one for Sunday-law violations limited freedom of religion. Judges had to decide such cases, and their decisions rested upon a series of related questions: Was the recognition and the protection of Christianity part of English common law? If so, did the common law apply in the United States? If so, to what extent? All depended upon the ultimate question: Was the United States a Christian nation?

Jurists and judges divided, and the result was a babel of conflicting legal opinions and decisions. Thus, St. George Tucker, a professor of

law at the College of William and Mary, argued that "liberty of conscience in matters of religion consists in the absolute and unrestrained
exercise of our religious opinions and duties . . . without the control or
intervention of any human power or authority whatsoever."[3] A New
York judge, William Jay (the son of John Jay), said essentially the
same thing in his charge to a grand jury: "This guaranty of freedom of
discussion . . . extends equally to religious and political topics. And it
is impossible to conceive any subject which we may not constitutionally discuss. The right is sacred, and no individuals whether magistrates or others can interfere to prevent its exercise."[4] But other judges
reasoned differently, using a double-barreled argument to sustain blasphemy laws. First, they ruled that such statutes, where they existed,
did not contradict the civil liberty guarantees of state constitutions.
Second, that blasphemy against Christianity was a crime at common
law, which transcends constitutional guarantees. To construe the New
York constitution "as breaking down the common law barriers against
licentious, wanton, and impious attacks upon Christianity itself," Kent
had ruled in the Ruggles case, "would be an enormous perversion of
its meaning."

In Pennsylvania one politician accused another of contempt for
Christianity, having "administered the sacrament to a dog." The accused politician sued for slander. The attorney for the defense argued
that it would be slander only if Christianity was part of the common
law of that state: "But what has the common law of England, in this
respect, to do with the common law of Pennsylvania? Does the Christian religion derive any support from our Constitution or our laws?
No."[5]

In 1813 Judge Hugh Brackenridge of the Pennsylvania Supreme
Court stated, "The Church establishment in *England* has become a
part of the common law. But was the common law in this particular, or
any part of it, carried with us in our emigration and planting a colony
in *Pennsylvania*? Not a particle of it."[6] However, his was a dissenting
opinion. Less than a decade later the same court declared that "no free
government now exists in the world, unless where Christianity is acknowledged, and is the religion of the country. Christianity is part of
the common law of this state. It is not proclaimed by the commanding
voice of any human superior, but expressed in the calm and mild ac-
cents of customary law. . . . It is the purest system of morality, the
firmest auxiliary, and the only stable support of all human laws."[7]

So frequently did judges make such rulings that in the 1840s a Philadelphia newspaper commented,

> We do not know what is generally meant when it is said that Christianity is part of the common law of the land. It is a very indefinite expression, which may mean much, or may mean little. It is a very convenient nose of wax, that may be shaped and twisted, and pointed at the will of any one who can lay his digits upon it. Does it mean that the state is thereby obligated to see that all men obey the laws which emanate from the founder of Christianity? If so they surely among these find baptism and the Lord's Supper standing prominent. Shall the state compel to the observance of these? And shall it decide who are proper subjects, and what is the proper mode of baptism? Shall it settle the long-mooted communion question, and tell who shall and who shall not be admitted to the Lord's table? If it is not allowed to intermeddle with these things which are so prominent in the scheme of Christianity, where are the limits in which it shall be confined? Before we admit the truth of the proposition that Christianity is part and parcel of the common law, we should like to know what the proposition means.[8]

Before the Civil War, individuals were prosecuted and convicted of blasphemy in Pennsylvania, New York, Delaware, and Massachusetts. In the Bay State, Abner Kneeland, who was so charged, reasoned that to be found guilty of blasphemy "would destroy the whole object of the provision in the [state] Bill of Rights." But the prosecutor responded that Christianity was part of the state constitution and the common law; and Jefferson, that "Virginian Voltaire," could not alter the law by his "imbecile dart" at Christianity. Judge Peter Thacher found the blasphemy law constitutional. "It would be an incredible thing if a race of men descended from the Puritan settlers of New England," said Thacher, "should in the lapse of a century and a half have so far departed from the sentiments of their fathers as to disregard all considerations when they were forming a political compact. . . . We find, however, that the framers of the constitution had not degenerated from the character of their ancestors." In a subsequent trial in 1838, Chief Justice Lemuel Shaw, agreeing with Thacher and citing Kent's decision in the Ruggles case, upheld the blasphemy law and sentenced Kneeland to prison.[9]

Jefferson and Story

Thomas Jefferson felt that judges were largely to blame for forging an alliance between government and Christianity. Before the American revolution he composed (in his commonplace book) an argument rebutting the assumption that Christianity was a part of the common law. He held to that principle all his life. In 1814, probably as a result of Kent's decision in the Ruggles blasphemy case, Jefferson wrote to John Adams, "Our judges . . . have been willing to lay the yoke of their own opinions on the necks of others; to extend the coercions of municipal law to the dogmas of their religion, by declaring that these make a part of the law of the land." [10] A decade later he thanked Major John Cartwright for his book, which included "a formal contradiction, at length, of the judiciary usurpation of legislative powers; for such the judges have usurped in their repeated decisions, that Christianity is a part of the common law. The proof of the contrary, which you have adduced, is incontrovertible." Adams agreed with Jefferson: "We think ourselves possessed or at least we boast that we are so of Liberty of conscience on all subjects and of the right of free inquiry and private judgment, in all cases and yet how far are we from these exalted privileges in fact. . . . I think such [blasphemy] laws a great embarrassment, great obstructions to the improvement of the human mind." [11]

Justice Joseph Story had long found Jefferson's argument offensive. In 1811, about the time he was appointed to the Supreme Court, Story penned an answer to Jefferson in *his* commonplace book (it was later published in *The American Jurist*). When he was appointed as Dane Professor of Law at Harvard University in 1829, Story seized the opportunity to again attack Jefferson's position:

> One of the beautiful boasts of our municipal jurisprudence is, that Christianity is a part of the Common Law, from which it seeks the sanction of its rights, and by which it endeavors to regulate its doctrines. And, notwithstanding the specious objection of one of our distinguished statesman, the boast is as true as it is beautiful. There never has been a period, in which the Common Law did not recognize Christianity as lying at its foundations. For many ages it was almost exclusively administered by those who held its ecclesiastical dignities. It now repudiates

every act done in violation of its duties of perfect obligation. It pronounces illegal every contract offensive to its morals. It recognizes with profound humility its holidays and festivals, and obeys them, as *dies non juridici*. It still attaches to persons believing in its divine authority the highest degree of competency as witnesses; and until a comparatively recent period, infidels and pagans were banished from the halls of justice as unworthy of credit.[12]

Story considered himself to be a strong advocate of the separation of church and state and a foe of religious bigotry. In his massive work *Commentaries on the Constitution*, published in 1833, Story praised the founding fathers for incorporating Article 6, section 3: "They knew, that bigotry was unceasingly vigilant in its strategems, to secure to itself an exclusive ascendancy over the human mind; and that intolerance was ever ready to arm itself with all the terrors of the civil power to exterminate those, who doubted its dogmas, or resisted its infallibility." The day of religious establishments was over. Religious tests for holding office were properly abandoned. Blasphemers were no longer burned at the stake. Yet, though these changes were wise and most welcome, though the common law was appropriately qualified, religious freedom in America had distinct limits. This was still a Christian country. Blasphemy against Christ or Christianity was a punishable offense; the testimony of atheists did not have equal weight in a court of law; Sunday laws were constitutional. "It is impossible for those who believe in the truth of Christianity, as a divine revelation," wrote Story in *Commentaries*, "to doubt, that it is the especial duty of government to foster and encourage it among all the citizens and subjects."[13]

Commentaries became a famous text, lauded in both America and England. Its message on the meaning and limits of religious freedom could be supplemented by Story's opinion in the case of *Vidal v. Girard's Executors* in 1844, which involved a bequest by Girard to the city of Philadelphia for the erection and support of a school for poor (white) orphans. The school would include teaching "the purest principles of morality" but would exclude all ministers "of any sect whatsoever" from affiliation with the institution. Story rejected Daniel Webster's argument for the plaintiffs, that the will was invalid as anti-Christian and therefore repugnant to the law of Pennsylvania. As Story wrote to his wife, "You know that I have ever been a sturdy defender of religious freedom of opinion, and I took no small pains to answer Mr. Webster's argument on this point, which went to cut down that freedom to a very narrow range." [14]

Story's opinion scarcely rates as a memorable exposition of religious freedom. He takes pains to exalt the "glorious principles" of "the Bible, and especially the New Testament." And again: "Where can the purest principles of morality be learned so clearly or so perfectly as from the New Testament? Where are benevolence, the love of truth, sobriety, and industry, so powerfully and irresistibly inculcated as in the sacred volume?" It would be a different case, Story noted, if someone wished to establish a school "for the propagation of Judaism, or Deism, or any other form of infidelity." That possibility "is not to be presumed to exist in a Christian country." Girard's will did not specifically forbid the teaching of Christianity; merely that it was not to be taught by ministers. Certainly there were laymen capable of performing that task. Moreover, Girard's will did not contemplate that Christianity was to be defiled or maligned at the school. If such were the case, the plaintiffs would be right, and the will would be void: "There must be plain, positive, and express provisions, demonstrating not only that Christianity is not to be taught, but that it is to be impugned or repudiated." For it is part of the common law to accept the "divine origin and truth" of Christianity, which is "not to be maliciously and openly reviled and blasphemed against." [15] Thus, speaking for a unanimous court, Story made the common law on Christianity, properly modified, part of federal jurisprudence.

The Conflict over Sunday Laws

In time the blasphemy laws became obsolete, although in several states they remain on the books and occasionally have been used to harass freethinking individuals. (Today, one scholar notes, "prosecutions [for blasphemy] are no more frequent than the sighting of snarks.") Sunday laws might have followed the same path. There was a considerable body of public opinion, at least outside New England, that was initially opposed to them.

Even within New England, Timothy Dwight admitted, there was occasional opposition. There the laws forbidding travel, amusement, or labor on Sunday were most severe, a fact that Dwight noted with some pride: "The Sabbath is observed in New England with a greater degree of sobriety and strictness than in any other part of the world." The Massachusetts law of 1792 declared that "irreligious or light-minded persons" must be kept from violating the Sabbath, "inasmuch as this manner of acting is contrary to their own interests as Christians; that furthermore it is of such a nature as to upset those who do not follow their example, and bring a real prejudice to the whole society by introducing the taste for dissipation and dissolute habits." One could find such dissipation in parts of New York State where, Dwight witnessed, Sunday is devoted "extensively to visiting, to amusement, and during the seasons of mowing and harvest, not infrequently to labor." Dwight realized that the subject was contentious. "Some of your countrymen, and not a small number of ours [in New England], regard this prohibition as an unwarrantable encroachment on personal rights, and complain of the laws with not a little bitterness," he wrote. "We without hesitation pronounce them to be right, founded on the law of God, and necessary to the preservation, as well as to the peaceful enjoyment, of that all important institution."[16] Many foreign visitors commented, as did de Tocqueville in 1831, on the "profound solitude" that reigned in Boston: "The whole movement of social life was suspended [on the Sabbath]. One can hear no sound of folk at work or at play, and not even that confused noise which constantly rises from any great city."[17]

All states had these laws (though none were so draconian as those of New England), and in many instances they were totally ignored. The Virginia Sunday law, for example, was mild: It forbade unnecessary labor or disturbances of religious services and provided for a fine of $1.67, which was rarely collected.[18] In western Pennsylvania, on the other hand, zealous Christians (mostly Presbyterian) organized "Moral Societies" in 1815 to stop profane swearing, intoxication, gambling, and violations of the Sabbath. Acting as vigilantes, they detained and arrested Sunday travelers. But when a famous lawyer, James Ross, sued them for unlawful arrest in the early 1820s and received considerable monetary damages for his client, the "Moral Societies" ceased these activities.[19] In upstate New York the debate took another form. Freight and passenger boats operated on the Erie Canal seven days a week, much to the distress of those (who were, again, mostly Presbyterian) Protestants who wished to ban the practice. The state legislature rejected a petition from Rochester to that effect, asking if the local citizens really wished to have hundreds of boatmen and travelers staying there on Sunday. The boatmen would only "drink grog and court Venus." Besides, it was bad for business. Sunday-law advocates joined forces, proclaimed a boycott of all "steamboats, stages, canal boats and livery stables" that operated on Sunday and formed a business venture of their own, the Pioneer Line, which would not operate on Sunday. What happened to it has been described by one scholar.

> By 1829 the Pioneer Line was a failure and a national laughingstock. But during its noisy and ineffectual career the Sabbatarian crusade split Rochester's ruling elite and wakened humbler men to the dangers of religious control. In the streets and on the canal, opposition to the Pioneer Line was immediate and sometimes violent. Pioneer handbills were torn down as fast as they could be put up, and strangers asking the way to the Pioneer offices were given bad directions. Rival boat crews made life miserable for men on the Pioneer packets. On one journey a Sabbath-keeping boat tried to pass one of the larger and slower freight boats. Men on the seven-day boat dumped two horses into the canal, cut in at locks, tore planks from the towpath to foul the Pioneer horses, cast loose a water-logged barge to obstruct passage of the faster boat, and cut the Pioneer tow rope three times.[20]

The debates became nationwide when, in 1828, a group of conservative merchants and old Federalists (including Judge Peter Thacher) meeting in New York City formed a General Union for Promoting the Observance of the Christian Sabbath. Their main goal was to stop the transportation and delivery of mail on Sunday. At their instigation church organizations and civic groups flooded Congress with petitions. "The people of these United States," read a memorial from Newark, New Jersey, "in their national capacity and character, constitute a Christian nation. If a Christian nation, then our Government is a Christian Government, a Government formed and established by Christians, and therefore bound by the word of God." From North Carolina came a similar message: "In a Christian community, where all the chartered rights and political institutions, as well as the legislative provisions of the country, recognize the authority of the Christian religion, your memorialists deem it unnecessary to employ any reasoning to prove that Sabbath breaking is sinful." It was indeed sinful, wrote the inhabitants of Williamson County, Tennessee, tempting "the God of the Sabbath to send down his fearful judgments upon our rising nation." The signers of a petition from Philadelphia reasoned that were they "Jews or Deists," they still would argue to cease Sunday mail delivery: "We would yield our convenience most cheerfully to that of a vast majority." The citizens of Alexandria, Virginia, quoted Blackstone in justification; those from Augusta, Maine, stated that without a Christian Sabbath "the influence of religious principle would soon be at an end"; and those from Boston cited a survey of 600 penitentiary inmates to make their point. Not one of the convicts had observed the Sabbath.[21]

But there were counterpetitions as well, some from the same towns and counties, praying Congress to retain Sunday mail delivery. From Newark: "[We are] induced to memorialize your honorable body at this time from a fear lest the reiterated efforts of bigotry and fanaticism should finally prevail. [We are] totally opposed to all attempts of the religious of any sect to control our consciences." From Philadelphia: "Your memorialists believe that if Congress possesses the power to designate what day shall be the Sabbath, and to define its appropriate duties, it would be equally within the scope of their authority to decide other disputed points." From Kentucky: "Is it because a large *majority* of the religious professors in the United States agree as to their Sabbath? Surely not; because the constitutional prohibitions intended to secure the rights of conscience were introduced solely for the purpose of protecting the rights of *minorities*." And a similar message from Windham, Vermont: "To all these, whether Jews, Mahometans, Pagans, or Christians, it is the design of the Constitution and the duty of the Legislature to extend equal rights and privileges." The legislatures of three states, Indiana, Illinois, and Alabama, filed concurring resolutions with Congress. The Indiana resolve stated:

> That we view all attempts to introduce sectarian influence into the councils of the nation as a violation of both the letter and the spirit of the constitution of the United States and of this State, and at the same time dangerous to our civil and religious liberties, inasmuch as those charters secure to every man the free exercise of his religion and the right to worship the Almighty God according to the dictates of his own conscience, and inasmuch as any legislative interference in matters of religion

would be an infraction of those rights; we, therefore, most respectfully remonstrate against any attempt, by a combination of one or more sects, to alter the laws providing for the transportation of mail, and against the passage of a law to regulate or enforce the observance of religious duties, or which may interfere with what belongs to the conscience of each individual: that all legislative interference in matters of religion is contrary to the genius of Christianity; and that there are no doctrines or observances inculcated by the Christian religion which require the arm of civil power either to enforce or sustain them: that we consider every connection between church and state at all times dangerous to civil and religious liberty: and further, that we cordially agree to and approve of the able report of the honorable R. M. Johnson.[22]

It was Senator Richard M. Johnson of Kentucky who argued that the Christian majority shall not impose its will upon the minority. He reminded Congress that the "Constitution regards the conscience of the Jew as sacred as that of the Christian."[23] Largely because of his efforts, the attempt to stop Sunday mail delivery failed. But that failure marked only the beginning of the campaign to strengthen Sunday laws all across the nation.

Garrison and Adams

The question of Sunday laws was of enormous significance to both sides. One felt that Christian civilization rested in the balance, for if these laws were to fall, so would Christianity. The flesh was weak, the allurements of sin many, and the arm of the state essential to support Christian morality. The other side felt that religious liberty rested in the balance, for if these laws were sustained, then constitutional protections were meaningless. The majority would, in effect, coerce obedience from dissenters who could not recognize Sunday as the Lord's day. As one historian has noted, the issue was debated with an intensity that "comes as a surprise to many twentieth-century Americans."[24] By the 1840s, evangelical Christians concentrated on cities, where growth had led to Sunday streetcar travel, amusements, business activities, and other secular pursuits. The broad spectrum of

Americans who had been initially opposed to these laws narrowed considerably before the Protestant assault. Mainline churches united in their favor, with Presbyterians (having absorbed a good percentage of Congregationalists) in the lead, Methodists firmly at their side, Episcopalians nodding an aristocratic assent, and Lutherans lagging behind (because so many German members of that church believed it was their historic right to visit beer taverns on Sunday).[25] Many Baptists, though historically committed to the separation of church and state, ultimately favored strict Sabbath legislation. Political lines wavered as well. In many states the degree of difference between Whigs and Democrats voting on Sunday laws was quite small.[26] Actively opposing these laws was a numerical minority of groups with sometimes antithetical interests: Seventh-Day Christian sects, Jews, atheists, liberal Protestants, and those Christian primitives who condemned the idea of a Sabbath as a perversion of a Jewish ceremonial that rightfully should have been abandoned as completely as circumcision.

Those who opposed Sunday laws were not always regarded as friends by Jews; nor were those in favor of such laws perceived to be hostile. William Lloyd Garrison, for example, drafted "An Appeal to the Friends of Civil and Religious Liberty," calling for an American Anti–Sunday-Law Convention to meet in Boston in 1848. Garrison excoriated the organizations in favor of Sunday laws as "animated by the spirit of religious bigotry and ecclesiastical tyranny." At the convention he declared, "Of all the assumptions on the part of legislative bodies, that of interfering between a man's conscience and his God is the most insupportable and the most inexcusable. For what purpose do we elect men? Is it to be our lawgivers on religious matters?" The convention adopted a resolution, "that if the Legislature may rightfully determine the *day* on which people shall abstain from labor for religious purposes, it may also determine the *place* in which they shall assemble, the *rites* and *ordinances* which they shall observe, the *doctrines* which they shall hear, the *teachers* which they shall have over them, and the peculiar *faith* which they shall embrace; and thus entirely subvert civil and religious freedom."[27]

Yet Garrison was one who believed that Protestantism had been corrupted by Jews and papists. He accused the editor of the *New England Spectator* of "groping in Jewish darkness." The ancient Jews were "oppressive and obdurate," guilty of "exclusiveness," a "cavilling" people whose "feet ran to evil." He charged them with "egotism and self-complacency" and stated that they deserved their "miserable dispersion in various parts of the earth, which continues to this day." The editor of Garrison's letters notes that he gave "no indication that the Old Testament was a Jewish book or that the prophets, whose sensitivity to injustice Garrison shared, were themselves Jewish."[28]

John Quincy Adams, on the other hand, maintained a public image of defending Jewish rights. (He confined his anti-Semitic comments to his private diary.) In 1833 a member of the British Parliament, Joseph Hume, in a speech to that body, paraphrased the contents of a letter he had received from Adams. Experience in America, Adams wrote, "bears testimony to the advantage of the admission of the Jews to civil rights and declares that no set of men can be better subjects." He also expressed a hope that other countries throughout Europe will follow the example of the United States "which have admitted Jews to a participation in the rights of free citizens."[29] Adams also thought of America as a Christian nation, and he devoted much effort to making it more so. In 1844 he served as president of a National Lord's Day Convention in Baltimore, the purpose of which was "to devise means for the promotion and sanctification of the Lord's day." It was attended by some 1,700 delegates from eleven states representing all major churches (but the majority were Presbyterian, Methodist, and Baptist). Typical of the resolutions that they passed was one requesting army officers not to exact military duties from soldiers on Sunday, and another—though not without debate, as some delegates feared "a collision or controversy with the national Legislature"—that regretted the fact that Congress "repeatedly [has] transacted public business on Sunday."[30] The time was not quite ripe for requesting a national law to enforce Sunday observance; that would come some decades later when Senator Henry W. Blair of New Hampshire introduced a "Bill to Secure to the People the Enjoyment of the First Day of the Week, Commonly Known as the Lord's Day, as a Day of Rest, and to Promote Its Observance as a Day of Religious Worship." John Quincy Adams would have approved.[31]

Certainly judges seemed to be paving the way for such a law by sustaining the constitutionality of state Sunday legislation. Quite frequently they supplemented what amounted to a religious decision (that America was a Christian nation) by adding a secular argument (that Sunday laws were a legitimate use of state police power). A minority of judges cut through this legal subterfuge and defied public opinion by declaring such laws to be unconstitutional, but the opponents of Sunday laws had few victories to cheer. By 1892 even the United States Supreme court declared that America was a "Christian nation."

Jewish Responses

There never was a unified Jewish response to Sunday laws. Quite the opposite; the issue proved to be as vexatious and divisive to Jews as it did to other Americans. Many Jews passively accepted these laws as a small price to pay for living in a nation that extended so many other precious freedoms. Some defended the laws as correct and equitable. "If the Israelites possessed a government of their own," wrote Mordecai Noah, "they would assuredly prohibit labor on the Sabbath day. It would be their duty to do so, enjoined by their own law. Why prohibit the Christians from enforcing the same regulations? The question ought not to be raised." [32] The courts merely fulfilled the maxim *salus populi suprema lex est*, Noah reasoned, and in a country of Christians there could be no other result. And some Jews promoted the idea—born in Germany in the 1830s—of holding their religious services on Sunday. The Sunday-Sabbath movement grew remarkably, especially among Reform Jews, despite the fact that a Reform Jewish rabbi, Isaac M. Wise, condemned the practice. Sunday was a Christian institution and Jews who justified its observance, he wrote in 1859, were guilty of "a bare faced and downright hypocrisy and lie." A few decades later he noted, "You can desecrate the Sabbath, but you cannot consecrate the Sunday." [33]

Isaac Leeser, more than any other Jewish spokesman, was concerned with and would settle for nothing less than complete legal and religious equality. As a Jew he could not sacrifice his Sabbath. As an American he insisted upon constitutional protection against the will of the majority. Leeser criticized not only judges who upheld Sunday laws, but Jewish shopkeepers who stayed open on Saturday and closed on Sunday. To do otherwise, they argued, was to break the law; to close two days was an economic sacrifice that they could not afford. Leeser called for that sacrifice. "The houses dedicated to God would not then be empty," he wrote, "because they who should be there are in their counting-houses or workshops, and then a true union of hearts and interests would form us into a strong community, able and willing to labor in the cause of Heaven, and we should not bear the reproach of the gentiles that we have forgotten our God, and then it would not be said with truth that by our misuse of liberty we have proved that freedom destroys national adhesion, and that only in adversity Israelites cling to the God of their fathers."[34] To accomplish this dream of union it was essential that Jews not be punished for keeping their Sabbath. There was more than a hint of jealousy, or admiration, in his remarks, for the strong union of faith, and willingness to sacrifice for that faith, displayed by the Seventh-Day sectarians.

The shared suffering and common goals of Jewish and Christian sabbatarians led to a measure of cooperation. Their periodicals contained numerous detailed accounts of their respective trials for violating the Sunday laws. The dockets were crowded with such trials—some were quite complex—involving licensing, property, and commerce, as well as civil rights. The following survey is a sampling of midnineteenth-century cases in several states.

South Carolina

In 1833 the South Carolina Supreme Court considered the case of two Columbia merchants, Alexander Marks, a Jew, and C. O. Duke, an avowed infidel (he had the temerity to say, "All days are alike to me, and therefore I will at all times pursue my business"), who were charged with violating a local ordinance forbidding stores from opening on Sunday. Marks and Duke claimed that the ordinance deprived them of religious liberty guaranteed by the state constitution. The state supreme court ruled otherwise. The ordinance, stated the court, "enjoins no profession of faith, demands no religious test, extorts no religious ceremony, confers no religious privilege or preference. . . . It requires no sacrifice on the part of any one, unless closing their doors and suspending their business be so considered."[35]

A Jewish merchant in Charleston, Solomon Benjamin, was charged with a similar offense in 1846; but a local judge, William Rice, declared the Sunday closing law unconstitutional as a "clear and palpable" violation of the defendant's freedom of religion. Rice was careful to point out that "no one entertains a more thorough conviction than myself that the Christian Sunday, or Lord's Day, should be kept in a becoming manner; and according to my religious faith, that it is a day peculiarly devoted and set apart to Christian worship, and upon which the ordinary secular employments of men, or in the language of the Church, all *servile works*, should be suspended." Moreover, Rice ruled that the government could legitimately exercise its authority (its police power) over many acts relating to Sunday. The law exempting slaves from labor on Sunday "is an eminently wholesome and humane provision and liable to no constitutional or well-founded objection." So, too, the law forbidding the issuing or service of legal process on Sunday: "The whole process of the law is of mere legal creation, and its machinery may be regulated, as to time and mode, by the law which creates it, without violating any natural rights." So, too, the ordinances punishing those "who disturb any religious assembly or congregation engaged in worship," because they make no reference to a particular day and in effect give "equal security to all sects and forms of religious worship without discrimination or preference." [36]

But, Rice asked, "by what authority" could the "civil power ordain, that on the day kept by Christians as a holy day or day of worship, peculiar to them, the Jew shall be made to keep in the same way, or to some extent at least, the Christian holy day; although, according to his religious faith, he is required to keep another and a different day, as sacred to religion, and in conscientious obedience to the command of the God he worships." Reverse the circumstances, said Rice, and the injustice is immediately apparent. Suppose Jews had a majority of the municipal council, could they "require by law on the part of the rest of the community, the same observance of the Jewish Sabbath, which is now required of them in regard to the Christian Sunday? If the Jew has no right to complain of the existing law, as in violation of his religious liberty, the Christian in the case supposed would have no other or further ground of objection." The constitution of South Carolina furnishes "ample security, and perhaps the only one, against undue encroachments upon religious liberty by the action of the legislative power . . . and to place at all times, and forever, freedom of conscience beyond the reach of any dominant or preponderating influence, which numbers may at any time give to a particular religious sect, or to any prevailing creed of the day." The Jewish Sabbath, Rice concluded, "kept with a fidelity which has outlived the downfall of their once glorious Temple, carried with their scattered people into every quarter of the globe, still claims the veneration, and is consecrated by the worship of the devout Israelite in our own happy land. Persecuted for so many centuries, the sport of tyranny and oppression, in so many climes, shall he not here at least be at liberty to worship God in freedom, and find peace and security upon the soil and under the Constitution of South Carolina?"[37]

Eight justices of the South Carolina Supreme Court concurred with the opinion of Judge John B. O'Neale, which reversed Rice and sustained the ordinance.

> The Lord's day, the day of the Resurrection, is to us who are called Christians, the day of rest after finishing a new creation. It is the day of the first visible triumph over death, hell and the grave! It was the birthday of the believer in Christ, to whom and through whom it opened up the way which, by repentance and faith, leads unto everlasting life and eternal happiness! On that day we rest and to us it is the Sabbath of the Lord—its decent observance in a Christian community, is that which ought to be expected.

> It is not perhaps necessary to the purposes of this case, to rule and hold that the Christian religion is part of the common law of South Carolina. Still it may be useful to show that it lies at the foundation of even the Article of the Constitution under consideration, and that upon it rest many of the principles and usages, constantly acknowledged and enforced in the courts of justice. . . .

> What gave to us this noble safeguard of religious toleration, which made the worship of our common Father as free and easy as the air we breathe, and his temple as wide, capacious and lofty as the sky he has spread above our heads? It was not that spirit of infidelity, which deified reason, denied God and was stained with more blood than ever flowed upon the altars of the Aztec Idols. It was Christianity robed in light, and descending as the dove upon our ancestors, which gave us this provision. It was that same spirit which, when the war of the revolution was about to commence, sanctified a fast, and prostrated a nation before the Lord of hosts, to ask his blessing and assistance. . . . Again, our law declares all contracts *contra bonos mores*, illegal and void. What constitutes the standard of good morals? Is it not Christianity? There certainly is none other. Say *that* cannot be appealed to, and I don't know what would be good morals. The day of moral virtue in which we live would, in an instant, if that

standard were abolished, lapse into the dark and murky night of
Pagan immorality. In this State, the marriage tie is indissolu-
ble—whence do we take that maxim? It is from the teaching of
the New Testament alone. In the courts over which we preside,
we daily acknowledge Christianity as the most solemn part of
our administration. A Christian witness, having no religious
scruples against placing his hand upon the Book, is sworn upon
the holy Evangelists—the books of the New Testament, which
testify of our Savior's birth, life, death and resurrection; this is
so common a matter that it is little thought of as an evidence of
the part which Christianity has in the common law. . . .

It is, however, fancied in some way this law is in derogation
of the Hebrew's religion, inasmuch as by his faith and this Statute, he is compelled to keep two Sabbaths. There is the mistake.
He has his own, free and undiminished. Sunday is to us our day
of rest. We say to him, simply, respect us, by ceasing on this
day from the pursuit of that trade and business in which you, by
the security and protection given to you by our laws, make great
gain. This is a mere police or municipal regulation.[38]

A number of Jews were outraged by O'Neale's decision. "An Hebrew" in a public letter to *The Occident*, called him "unquestionably a
fanatic," "an unsafe judge on all questions bearing upon his own bigoted notions," and objected "to the whole tone of the decision, and the
spirit in which it was written. The Judge, throughout, treats Jews as
though they were not his equals—his fellow-citizens . . . I protest
against these terms, '*you*,' '*us*,' '*our laws*.' Such language is unworthy
of an American judge." If the opening of a store on Sunday is an "act
of licentiousness" that shocks the "moral sense" of Christians, the author asked,

I put it to Judge O'Neale . . . whether I would not much more
shock that "moral sense" if I were to denounce the trinity, and
the atonement, as blasphemous and immoral? If such be the law,
how do the Jews in this country stand? The country may be
flooded with denunciations against the Jewish religion, and no
principle of the law will be found to check the torrent of abuse,
of slander, and of falsehood; whilst ample protection may be
given to Christianity from any attack that would 'shock the
moral sense' of Christians. Is this no 'discrimination,' no 'pref-

erence'? Under this rule of law, I suppose, Judge O'Neale would
. . . grant an injunction to restrain the publication of *The Occident* on the ground that it was anti-Christian and therefore *contra bonos mores* and in violation of the law of the land.[39]

"An American Jew" also took pen in hand, citing O'Neale's decision as "alarming evidence" that "fanaticism has spread itself over the land" but confining his letter to a theological rebuttal of O'Neale's "blasphemous" assertion "that Christianity is the only standard of good morals."[40] O'Neale took the time to respond to the latter criticism, saying "that the thought of offending them, or deprecating their religion, never entered my mind! *The Bible is a part, and a large part, of Christianity.* In asserting Christianity to be the only standard of good morals, *the Bible* was of course *as much that standard* as the New Testament. . . . How I, *not born a Jew*, could say otherwise, than that Christianity was the only standard *known* to me of good morals, is hard for me to conceive."[41]

Some Jews came to O'Neale's defense. Mordecai M. Noah commented in his newspaper, *Sunday Times and Noah's Weekly Messenger*, that it was "a very able opinion" with which "we entirely agree." The Sunday law was a mere local or police regulation: "We cannot . . . perceive how liberty of conscience is to be invaded. It does not say to the Hebrew, 'You shall not keep holy the seventh day'; but merely declares that you shall not disturb the Christian by business or labor on his Sabbath. We can see nothing wrong in this. . . . Respect to the laws of the land we live in, is the first duty of good citizens of all denominations."[42]

Pennsylvania

Noah's view probably was more representative of Jewish opinion, but Leeser remained adamant. He reminded his readers that a case similar to the one in South Carolina "will come up in the Supreme Court of Pennsylvania," which involved "several Seventh-day Baptists of Franklin county, who are under indictment for laboring on the first day of the week. Should they gain the case in state court, it will exercise a strong moral influence all over the Union."[43] Leeser had hopes. Although some Pennsylvania judges previously had pronounced Christianity a part of the common law of the state, others had denied that fact, and still others had rendered halfway interpretations, as in an 1829 case: "Christianity is indeed recognized as the predominant religion of the country, and for that reason are not only its institutions, but the feelings of its professors, guarded against insult from reviling or scoffing at its doctrines. So far it is the subject of special favor. But further the law does not protect it. Happily, it neither needs nor endures the patronage of temporal authority."[44] There was no telling how the court would decide in 1848.

Leeser was wrong, however. The Supreme Court of Pennsylvania in *Specht v. Commonwealth* unanimously confirmed the conviction of the Seventh-Day Baptists for working (farming) on Sunday. Yet the intriguing fact was that the two opinions making up the decision were contradictory in nature. One judge based his ruling on state police power; the other on Christianity. The author of an article in the *Democratic Review* pointed this out by placing the words of the two justices in parallel columns.

JUDGE BELL	JUDGE COULTER
It is still essentially but a *civil regulation*, made for the government of man as a member of society; and obedience to it may properly be enforced by penal sanctions. . . . It cannot be said a primary object of the act was authoritatively to assert the supremacy of Sunday as of divine appointment. . . . In this aspect of the statute, there is therefore nothing in derogation of the constitutional inhibition.	I wish it to be distinctly understood, that I believe the laws constitutional because they guard the Christian Sabbath from profanation, and in the language of the act of 1794, prohibit work or worldly employment on the Lord's Day. We are a Christian people and state . . . and I do not recognize the right of legislation to make a day of secular cessation from labor, independent of the Christian Sabbath.[45]

The author concluded that "one of the judgments must necessarily be erroneous; and both must be partially wrong, unless one is totally so." He disposed of Judge Bell's logic by establishing that the Sunday law was Christian in intent and in application. He ridiculed Judge

Coulter's logic because it was "founded on the vague idea that a state, like an individual, if without any religion, is but a mighty Infidel . . . 'A *Christian* state'! Why, it has only a corporate existence. It has neither a soul to be saved, nor even a body to be baptized. It can neither join the 'communion-table' of the pious below, nor the chorus of departed saints above. 'A *Christian* state'! How perfectly incongruous the conception. As well a Christian engine or a Christian clock!"[46]

A few years later, in 1854, Leeser took heart because the Pennsylvania Supreme Court split, three to two, in affirming the conviction of an "omnibus driver" in Pittsburgh for violating the Sunday laws. The majority decision rested on the primacy of Christianity in the lives of Pennsylvanians, which included "the right to rear a family with a becoming regard for the institution of Christianity, and without compelling them to witness hourly infractions of one of its fundamental laws." But the dissenting opinions were vigorously stated.

> The government has no more authority on this question of observing the first day of the week than it has on the other disputes of polemic theology. It may as well attempt to make men unanimous on the duties of prayer, devout meditation, baptism, or the eucharist, as on this. It is no doubt very desirable that we should all be of one mind on subjects which interest us deeply. But how shall such a consummation be effected? The experiment of legal force has been fully tried, and is a flat failure. . . . Of all blunders the most preposterous is the effort to advance religious truth by state favor, and of all tyranny the most brutal, blind, and revolting is that which punishes a man for the sincere convictions of his heart.[47]

The following year, one of the above dissenters, on circuit, overturned the conviction of a lockkeeper of the Schuylkill Navigation Company for opening the canal locks on Sunday.[48] Yet the full court continued to uphold the convictions of Sunday-law violators. "Destroy this day," ruled the supreme court in 1859, in a case involving the conductor of a streetcar on Sunday, "and a revolution of the most astounding character is produced [, one which] must shake Christianity itself."[49]

The Philadelphia *Public Ledger* took obvious delight in reporting the arrest in Pittsburgh of the coach driver of the chief justice of the Pennsylvania Supreme Court for "driving the family of that distinguished legal luminary to church on Sunday morning." The arrest was ordered by the mayor of Pittsburgh, who stated that "what is sauce for the goose is sauce for the gander." The chief justice might claim that going to church is a necessity; but going in a carriage is not so long "as he has a pair of stout legs to carry him." The *Public Ledger* commented:

> If any victim is to be made to the straight-laced interpretation given to an antiquated and ridiculous law, which deprives citizens of the religious freedom guaranteed to them by the Constitution of the United States, we do not know a martyr more fit for the sacrifice than the Chief Justice of Pennsylvania. It is the Court of which he is the chief which have decided, in spite of the organic law of the land, that Christianity is part of the common law of the State, which of course ignores the constitutional right of every Hebrew citizen, and renders him liable to pains and penalties for not observing the customs and observances of other religious persuasions. It has also decided that the Puritan Sabbath is the Christian Sabbath, which is denied by many other Christian sects.[50]

Pennsylvania judges continued to tack between secular and religious justifications of Sunday laws, with the latter predominating. In 1867 Judge William Strong, at that time president of the National Reform Association, issued an injunction to stop the Union Passenger Railway Company in Philadelphia from operating on Sunday because it was unnecessary and deprived Christians of their right to a quiet Sabbath. He dismissed the arguments of defendants that streetcar travel was necessary to doctors who visited the sick on Sunday; and for the poor to escape their "badly ventilated neighborhoods." Strong's ruling even included the legal argument that church pews were real property, purchased at prices "equal to the value of many small farms," and that their value might be impaired or destroyed by the noise of streetcars.[51]

Virginia

There were no significant Sunday-law cases in Virginia at midcentury because the state law was changed to accommodate sabbatarians. For decades the law had remained unused and had become virtually obsolete, when in 1845 the city of Richmond passed an ordinance "for the more effectual suppression of Sabbath-breaking." The motivation for this ordinance had nothing to do with Jews. It was designed, as a contemporary stated, because of the "vicious popula- tion of slaves and free negroes . . . let loose upon the community in idleness . . . with an unlimited scope to indulge their illicit propen- sities."[52] Crime would disappear by closing down the Sunday opera- tion of bakeries, barber shops, vegetable markets, and other businesses where blacks congregated. Several Jewish merchants were arrested, and a number of them filed a petition of protest: They had fought in the Revolution, they had "snatched up arms at the first alarm, and at the memorable attack on the frigate Chesapeake," and they were honored to do so, for "they were part of the legislative power, alike in the eye of the law, not distinguished by any disqualification because of their be- lief or religious conduct." The new ordinance, they regretted, was a "manifestation of the sectarian spirit, which deems it paramount to bring every one to its own mode of thinking [, and it] is but the begin- ning of a revolution backwards, to abridge the rights of individuals, which have been opened as wide as the gates of mercy by the sages of the Revolution." Moreover, the ordinance "is in contravention of the Constitution and Bill of Rights of this State, by assigning to Sunday- keeping Christians more legal protection than is accorded to Jews and the Seventh-Day Baptists; they therefore feel almost confident that if an appeal were properly brought before the highest judicial authority of the State, your ordinance would be annulled."[53]

The Richmond city council appointed a committee headed by Joseph Mayo (the city attorney and later mayor). "We are truly rejoiced," wrote Leeser, "that the good cause of the fullest liberty of conscience has found so able an expounder."[54] Mayo's report convinced the coun- cil to rescind the ordinance. Meanwhile, two Jews, Jacob A. Levy and Jacob Ezekiel, petitioned the state legislature to repeal or modify the state Sunday law, which, they noted, "though enacted by a legal ma- jority of the Legislature, owes its origin more to a thoughtless acquies- cence of the members to the usual opinions prevailing around them, than by any well founded agreement this act has with the absolute equality of all the citizens guaranteed by the Constitution." In conclu- sion, they wrote,

> your petitioners wish it to be distinctly understood that they ask for no special legislation; they desire no favor for themselves

which is denied other citizens; they merely desire that they should be upon the same footing, as Jews, with those who are Christians; they ask for no protection for the seventh day, which they conscientiously believe and can defend by historical data, as being the original Sabbath; but they as freemen respectfully demand that neither shall the Christian Sunday obtain any legal sanction, at least to the degree of inflicting penalties on those whose conscience does not give it any sacredness, and they believe that religion of all sorts will prosper more by being divested of legislative interference.[55]

At a meeting of the state legislature in 1849 for the purpose of recodifying the laws, Joseph Mayo was instrumental in having the Sunday law amended to exempt from penalty "any person who conscientiously believed that the seventh day of the week ought to be observed as the Sabbath . . . provided he does not compel a slave, apprentice, or servant not of his belief to do secular work or business on Sunday, and does not on that day disturb any other person." The amendment was not passed without debate. One legislator who spoke in its favor told the state senate that

he did not represent Israelites or Seven Day Baptists. He did not know of one in his district; but as an individual, and as a senator, he would enter his solemn protest against this mode of legal proscription—denying to individuals or sects the enjoyment of their religion. . . . He had witnessed with pleasure and astonishment the great sacrifice of pecuniary interest on the part of Jews residing in other cities, in the observance of [their Sabbath]. In doing so they were compelled, either from choice or from the force of public opinion, to observe also the Christian Sabbath. He thought they could not be induced to submit, with such calm resignation, to this sacrifice of worldly interest, if it was not the result of an overwhelming sense of moral and religious obligation.[56]

Leeser never mentioned that the original Sunday law in Virginia had been endorsed by Jefferson and Madison (he might not have known it).[57] Instead, he wrote that he loved "this old commonwealth; it is the home of generous feelings, and the seat of true liberty of conscience; this has been frequently proved, especially by the late act to repeal all punishments for not observing Sunday on the part of those who keep the seventh day Sabbath; for though at one time misled to enact an exceptional law, that State repealed it as soon as the injustice was made manifest."[58]

Ohio

Within a few years Leeser had changed his mind. There was one option preferable to Virginia's method of exempting "conscientious" Jews from Sunday laws: to have no Sunday laws at all. Ohio judges had come to the same conclusion as Virginia legislators, that conscientious Jews were exempt. But in 1858 a Jewish ice-dealer in Cincinnati had been convicted for selling ice on Sunday. Though he "abstained from worldly pursuits" on Saturday, his sons did not. They sold ice on Saturday and turned the profits over to their father. A Jewish correspondent told Leeser that the judicial finding was fair; it was certainly better than the laws in Pennsylvania and in South Carolina, where Jews were compelled to observe the Lord's day. Leeser disagreed. However hypocritical was the ice-dealer, "one must dissent most emphatically from the assumption of the right on the part of civil tribunals of setting themselves up as vindicators of our religion." How could the courts tell who was and who was not pious? Were they to enter the ring of theological controversy? Did they have a right to do so? Leeser was convinced that the Ohio judge "cared . . . nothing for ice being sold on Saturday, and he only punished its being done on Sunday; wherefore not the violation of the Jewish principle was the object of the law's vengeance, but the transgression of a statute which exacts rest on the first day of the week." If it is unconstitutional for the government to favor one religion over another, then Sunday laws were unconstitutional. To say that Sunday laws "are merely municipal, and not religious" is "absurd." To say that these laws protect the laboring classes is a "fallacy." What they protect is "the protestant, trinitarian, Christian churches . . . by the compulsory enforcement of rest and leisure on the day selected by them for worship."[59]

California

In every prominent case, except one, Leeser noted, the highest state tribunals had "decided adversely to the *natural* right of freedom" by sustaining Sunday laws. That celebrated exception occurred in California, where the question of Sunday laws was a volatile issue in the 1850s. Many easterners were scandalized by the California lifestyle, especially by the desecration of the Sabbath in that new state. Hinton R. Helper described Sunday there "as a day of hilarity and bacchanalian sports" where "horse-racing, cock-fighting, cony-hunting, card-playing, theatrical performances and other elegant amusements are freely engaged in."[60] Another visitor to San Francisco remarked that "the shops of the Jew," and even "a few stores of the sons of the pilgrims, the drinking saloons, and other public resorts, are open and filled as on other days."[61] When the famous theologian Horace Bushnell delivered a lecture entitled "Society and Religion: A Sermon for California" at the First Congregational Church of San Francisco in 1856, he told his audience that the practice of Sunday in that state, "instead of purifying the whole week, is a day that corrupts more virtue, ruins more character, than all the other six days together." The influx of "foreign" immigrants in California, he believed, brought a flood of crime. The lack of law and order would not be solved until a Christian Sunday was imposed by the legislature. "Not a Jewish Sabbath," he thundered, "and still less that mongrel day which is a cross between the pleasures of vice and sanctities of religion." What the people needed was the "drill of law" to tone their minds "to duty." If his audience truly desired "to have laws and have them executed; to have justice, personal security, and public order," then they must realize that they "can have no such thing without a Christian Sabbath."[62]

Bushnell would not have approved of the Sunday law the California legislature enacted in 1858: It exempted taverns, inns, restaurants, hotels, boardinghouses, and livery stables. (Grogshops tried to masquerade as inns or taverns, and there was considerable wrangling over definitions wherever officials attempted to enforce the law's provisions.)[63] But the law did proclaim a "Christian Sabbath," and its prohibition of certain businesses or sales did not allow exceptions for conscientious sabbatarians. Soon thereafter a Jewish merchant from Sacramento, M. Newman, was convicted in a lower court for violating the law by selling clothes on Sunday. The lower court found the law constitutional because the legislature "can set aside" any day of the week "from motives of public policy."

Carried to the state supreme court, one of the prosecutors, District Attorney R. F. Morrison, in oral presentation, "defied those who represent the other side to show any decision that was opposed to the mass of authority, gathered from all portions of the Union" in support of Sunday laws. Morrison cited in particular the opinions of Judge Bell in the Pennsylvania case of *Specht v. Commonwealth*, and that of Judge O'Neale in the South Carolina case of Solomon Benjamin. All judicial precedents favored the law. The defense attorneys countered with the argument that these precedents should be ignored. "If decisions have been made in other states of the Union," stated D. W. Welty, "this was no guide for California. She was remote from them, isolated, peculiar in her relations, and should lay down, as a pioneer State, a position in this respect for herself." His co-counsel, Solomon Heydenfeldt, reasoned along the same lines: "When judges in the East had decided that Sunday laws were constitutional, they had resorted to subterfuges." Both defense attorneys maintained that the issue was not toleration but religious liberty, which the California Sunday law impaired. The law was discriminatory and in obvious violation of several provisions of the California constitution. Said Heydenfeldt, "If this be the law, he could go to Russia and get the same kind of toleration. Toleration did not exclude preference. They had toleration in England, but they had also preference. . . . Governmentally considered, this was not a Christian country, and the counsel instanced a case in our relations with Tripoli, to show that it could not be so considered."[64]

Heydenfeldt brought to the legal defense a moral fervor born of personal involvement, because he was Jewish, and the added prestige attached to the fact that he had recently been a member of the California Supreme Court. But probably more influential with Chief Justice David Terry, one may speculate, was their shared southern background.[65] Whatever the reason, Terry, speaking for a majority of the court, adopted the logic of the defense. "While we entertain a profound respect for the Courts of our sister States," he ruled, "we do not feel called upon to yield our convictions of right to a blind obedience to precedent." Because he could not cite judicial precedents, Terry quoted extensively from the Sunday mail report of Richard Johnson. He went on to ask: How could anything people do six days of the week, which is not only "peaceable and lawful, but praiseworthy and commendable," be converted into a penal offense on the seventh? Surely there were aspects of life that the legislature must regulate for our health and well-being: the sale of drugs, the discharge of firearms, the practice of medicine, etcetera. The Sunday law was not in this category. It could not be justified upon the basis of necessity. The prosecution contended that society requires a day of rest, "that mankind are in the habit of working too much . . . and that without compulsion they will not seek the necessary repose. . . . This is to us a new theory." And it was as irrelevant as it was erroneous. "The truth is, however much it may be disguised, that this one day of rest is a purely religious idea." Religion motivated its enactment. Such has been the case "in most of the states," where the "aid of the law to enforce its observance has been given under the pretence of a civil, municipal, or police regulation." To Terry the Sunday law was clearly unconstitutional.

> In a community composed of persons of various religious denominations, having different days of worship, each considering his own as sacred from secular employment, all being equally considered and protected under the Constitution, a law is passed which in effect recognizes the sacred character of one of these days, by compelling all others to abstain from secular employment, which is precisely one of the modes in which its observance is manifested and required by the creed of that sect, to which it belongs as a Sabbath. Is not this a discrimination in favor of the one? Does it require more than appeal to one's common sense to decide that this is a preference; and when the Jew or Seventh Day Christian complains of this, is it any answer to say, Your conscience is not constrained, you are not compelled to worship, or to perform religious rites on that day, nor forbidden to keep holy the day which you esteem as a Sabbath? We think not, however high the authority which decides otherwise.[66]

Judge Peter Burnett concurred. "Had the act made Monday, instead of Sunday, a day of compulsory rest, the constitutional question would have been the same," he wrote. "The fact that the Christian *voluntarily* keeps holy the first day of the week does not authorize the Legislature to make that observance *compulsory*."[67]

The dissenting judge, Stephen J. Field, was the son of a Connecticut Congregational minister. His biographer states that Field was raised in a home in which "the Sabbath . . . was observed with almost Jewish strictness."[68] In California Field moved from Congregationalism to Presbyterianism and then to Episcopalianism. Theological distinctions between these churches did not interest him. Each represented order, stability, and respectability, which Field was determined to preserve. "Christianity is the prevailing faith of our people," wrote Field in his dissent, "it is the basis of our civilization; and that its spirit should infuse itself into and humanize our laws, is as natural as that the national sentiment of liberty should find expression in the legislation of the country." Yet Field attempted to mask his own religious motives. He argued that whether the intention of the legislators was or was not a religious one—the record indicates that it was—had no bearing. Nor did the use of the words "Christian Sabbath" in the law. It was simply a "civil regulation," which cannot "be converted into a religious institution because it is enforced on a day which a particular religious sect regards as sacred." Selling clothes on Sunday is scarcely a religious act. The law deals with "business matters, not religious duties. . . . It makes no discrimination or preference between the Hebrew and Gentile, the Mussulman and Pagan, the Christian and Infidel." The entire civilized world "has given the sanction of law" to this beneficent rule of rest on Sunday: "Upon no subject is there such a concurrence of opinion, among philosophers, moralists, and statesmen of all nations, as on the necessity of periodic cessations from labor."[69]

Three years later the California legislature reenacted substantially the same Sunday law, and the state supreme court, made up of different judges—including Field—sustained it.

The Christian Nation Decision

Terry's argument became a legal curiosity that was cited in many other state cases by attorneys arguing to strike down Sunday laws, to no avail. Judges followed Field's line of reasoning: We are a Christian people, but Sunday laws are civil, not religious, and do not violate freedom of religion. Thus, in 1867 the Texas Supreme Court ruled that "the vast majority of our people profess a belief in the Christian religion. . . . The followers of that faith have from its earliest existence and foundation regarded Sunday as a day of rest. . . . And, as a civil regulation, it has been considered important for the physical well-being of society that Sunday be observed as a day of rest." The Georgia Supreme Court stated in 1871, "The law fixes the day recognized as the Sabbath day all over Christendom, and that day, by Divine injunction, is to be kept holy—'on it thou shalt do no work.' The Christian Sabbath is a civil institution, older than our government." The Illinois Supreme Court in 1883 stated, "Although it is no part of the functions of our system of government to propagate religion, and to enforce its tenets, when the great body of the people are Christians, in fact or sentiment, our laws and institutions must necessarily be based upon and embody the teachings of the Redeemer of mankind." The Nebraska Supreme Court declared in 1892, "Christianity is woven into the web and woof of free government and but for it free government would not have existed, because no other system has been able to check the selfishness, arrogance, cruelty and covetousness of the race. . . . As a Christian people, therefore, jealous of their liberty and desiring to preserve the same, the State has enacted certain statutes, which, among other things, in effect, recognize the fourth commandment, and the Christian religion, and the binding force of the teachings of the Savior." (The case involved playing baseball on Sunday.)[70]

The United States Supreme Court had upheld state Sunday laws as a valid exercise of civil authority long before Stephen J. Field moved to that court. He continued the line of argument, but it was his nephew and fellow judge on the Supreme Court, David J. Brewer, who wrote the decision that capped and placed an official stamp of approval on the opinions of his judicial forebears. The son of a Christian missionary to Turkey, Brewer felt compelled to add an unmistakable endorsement of the primacy of Christianity. In an 1892 case, *Holy Trinity Church v. United States*, involving the contract labor of aliens, he included an extensive obiter dictum through which marched numerous citations of English and colonial history, the early state constitutions requiring Protestant oaths for holding office, Chancellor Kent's words in the Ruggles case and Judge Story's in the Girard case, the universality of Sunday laws ordering the "cessation of all secular business," the labors of Christian charities and Christian missions "in every quarter of the globe," and the volume of "unofficial declarations" added "to the mass of organic utterances," all of which led to only one conclusion: "that this is a Christian nation."[71]

Some years later, in a series of talks entitled "The United States a

Christian Nation," Brewer stated that Christianity stands for patriotism, business honesty, liberty, the rights of man, education, charity, peace, temperance, and purity of the home. No longer, apparently, did the threats to Christianity come from a triumvirate of Jews, Turks, and infidels. Rather, "it is Mormonism, Mohammedanism, and heathenism," he believed, "which have proclaimed polygamy and debased women from the sacred place of wife to the lower level of concubine." Christianity should be treated with the same respect accorded to the national flag. And he admitted that although judges upheld Sunday laws on a secular basis, their motivation essentially was religious: "It is true in many of the decisions, this . . . day is said to be authorized by the police power. . . . At the same time, through a large majority of them, there runs the thought of its being a religious day."[72]

End of the Century

For the hundreds of thousands of Jewish immigrants who began to arrive at the close of the nineteenth century, America was a blessed land of liberty. Here there were no pogroms, no marching mobs shouting anti-Semitic slogans, as in Europe. Yet here there was an enigma, a contradiction, because American leaders claimed the United States to be both a country of religious equality and a Christian nation. Which was it? How could it be both?

In 1885 the Austro-Hungarian government refused to accept the appointment of an American diplomat, Anthony Keiley of Virginia, because his wife was Jewish. "The position of a foreign envoy wedded to a Jewess by civil marriage," the United States was informed, "would be untenable and even impossible in Vienna." Secretary of State Thomas F. Bayard responded that the United States could not "suffer an infraction" of its fundamental belief in religious equality, for to do so "would lead to a disfranchisement of our citizens because of their religious belief, and thus impair or destroy the most important end which our constitution of Government was intended to secure." President Grover Cleveland explained to Congress that the arguments of the Austro-Hungarian government "could not be acquiesced in, without violation of my oath of office and the precepts of the Constitution."[73]

A few years later, Protestant groups pressured Congress to deny appropriations for the 1893 World's Columbia Exposition in Chicago unless it closed on Sunday. Led mostly by Presbyterians, Congregationalists, and Methodists, and their allied groups such as the Christian Endeavor Union, the National Reform Association, the Ministerial Alliance, the American Sabbath Union, and the Women's Christian Temperance Union, they threatened to use their combined votes to defeat any politician who voted otherwise. Congressmen admitted, as did Senator Joseph Hawley of Connecticut, that the bill was "founded on religious belief." When Congressman John Pattison of Ohio said, "We but voice the sentiment of the many millions of Christian people and also at least nine-tenths of the American people," Albert Hopkins of Illinois asked, "What would the gentleman do with those who have Saturday as their Sabbath?"

Pattison: "There are very few of those . . ."

Hopkins: "But their conscientious scruples are as sacred to them as those who desire the doors to be closed on Sunday."

An unnamed congressmen told a reporter for the Chicago *Daily Post*, "The reason we shall vote for it is, I will confess to you, a fear that, unless we do so, the church folks will get together and knife us at the polls."[74] The law passed easily.

So the signals were mixed, as they have always been in American history: the government on one occasion defending the constitutional equality of all its citizens regardless of religious belief, and on another by passing a law denying the equal rights of sabbatarians and non-Christians. And the response of Jews was mixed, as it frequently had been throughout the century, ranging the entire spectrum of reactions from discreet silence to secular indifference to assimilationist strategies to an insistence on preserving their constitutional rights. Some followed the advice of Sadie American, the secretary of the National Council of Jewish Women, who in 1900 "denounced the maintenance of the Jewish Sabbath as indicating a lack of progressiveness and as a manifestation of narrowmindedness, and she advocated the substitution of the Christian Sunday."[75] Others continued to follow the standards set by Isaac Leeser, though in the particular example of challenging the legality of Sunday laws their cause seemed futile.

As the twentieth century advanced, the wall of separation between church and state would be patched, breached, and cemented over, time and again. Those who labor at that task should remember that they stand on a foundation of similar efforts that stretch back to the beginning of American national history. The concern of a small number of Jews was an important factor that caused other Americans to think about the meaning of religious freedom and, in many instances, to broaden its definition.

NOTES

Chapter One

1. Martin E. Marty, *Righteous Empire: The Protestant Experience in America* (New York, 1970), 39.
2. Anson P. Stokes, *Church and State in the United States*, 3 vols. (New York, 1950), 1: 292.
3. Cecilia M. Kenyon, ed., *The Antifederalists* (Indianapolis, 1966), lxix.
4. Naphtali Phillips to James McAllister, 24 October 1868, in "The Federal Parade of 1788," *American Jewish Archives* 7 (January 1955): 65–67.
5. "Observations on the Federal Procession on the Fourth of July, 1788, in the City of Philadelphia," *The American Museum* 4 (1788): 77.
6. How many Jews were there? What percentage were they of the total population? The figures are rough guesses at best, and even the official census of 1790 (showing a total population of 3,900,000) is not trustworthy, because the census undercounted. Readers are free to do their own mathematical calculations, but, as my colleague, Dr. Patricia Cohen, reminds me, "dividing the Jewish population by the total population" is not "the most meaningful way to convey a sense of the size or importance of the Jewish community. Jews were not distributed evenly throughout the population."
7. John Hampden Pleasants, editor of the Richmond, Virginia, *Constitutional Whig*, introduced the first published essay by Isaac Leeser with a glowing endorsement (9 Janury 1829): "Whether we view the Jews historically or religiously—as one of the earliest nations of the earth, still existing in observation of their ancient usages—or as the chosen people of God, selected in the first instance to receive the dispensations of his will, and after, to sustain for ages, his wrath and displeasure—the view is calculated to fill us with sentiments of awe, admiration, sympathy and reverence. When we see one of this people, and remember that we have been told by good authority, that he is an exact copy of the Jew who worshipped in the Second Temple two thousand years ago—that his physiognomy and religious opinions—that the usages and customs of his tribe are still the same, we feel that profound respect which antiquity inspires" (Herbert T. Ezekiel and Gaston Lichtenstein, *The History of the Jews of Richmond from 1769 to 1917* [Richmond, 1917], 56).
8. Arthur A. Chiel, "Ezra Stiles and the Jews: A Study in Ambivalence," in *A Bicentennial Festschrift for Jacob Rader Marcus*, ed. Bertram W. Korn (New York, 1976), 66, 71–72. Stiles's main concern, as he stated in a 1783 sermon, "The United States Elevated to Glory and Honor," was the "growing idea" that "deists, and men of indifferentism to all religion, are the most suitable persons for civil office, and most

proper to hold the reigns of government" (John W. Thornton, *The Pulpit of the American Revolution* [Boston, 1860], 488–89).

9. Edwin Wolf and Maxwell Whiteman, *The History of the Jews of Philadelphia from Colonial Times to the Age of Jackson* (Philadelphia, 1956), 149.

10. Dwight was referring to Judah Monis, an instructor in Hebrew at Harvard, who had been converted to Christianity in 1722. Dwight recorded the tombstone inscription, which included the couplet: "A native branch of Jacob see / Which, once from off its olive broke / Regrafted from the living tree / Of the reviving sap partook" (Timothy Dwight, *Travels in New England and New York*, 4 vols. [Cambridge, Mass., 1969], 1: 270). The Society for Evangelizing the Jews included among its officers Elias Boudinot, Stephen Van Rensselaer, and John Quincy Adams, who was shortly to be appointed secretary of state.

11. Philadelphia *Sunday Dispatch*, 28 May 1871, in *A Documentary History of the Jews in the United States*, ed. Morris U. Schappes (New York, 1971), 552.

12. Jonathan D. Sarna, "The American Jewish Response to Nineteenth-Century Christian Missions," *The Journal of American History* 68 (June 1981): 51.

13. In 1840 Isaac Leeser noted that "the present age is one of great danger to Judaism . . . the spread of infidel indifference which scorns the dictates of religion, the acts of rulers and societies who endeavor to make it *worth while* for the Jew to become an apostate, have all combined to withdraw many from the active pursuit of the Jewish faith" (*The Claims of the Jews to an Equality of Rights* [Philadelphia, 1841], 81).

14. Theodore Sizer, ed., *The Autobiography of Colonel John Trumbull* (New Haven, 1953), 174–75.

15. William G. McLoughlin, ed., *Isaac Backus on Church, State, and Calvinism: Pamphlets, 1754–1789* (Cambridge, Mass., 1968), 436. Backus approved Article 6, section 3 of the Constitution, but he did not demand an amendment securing religious freedom.

16. Thomas O'Brien Hanley, ed., *The John Carroll Papers* 3 vols. (Notre Dame, 1976), 1: 259.

17. Frederic Chase, *A History of Dartmouth College*, 2 vols. (Cambridge, Mass., 1891), 1: 661.

18. E. C. in *Gazette of the United States*, 6–9 May 1789.

19. Lester J. Cappon, ed., *The Adams–Jefferson Letters*, 2 vols. (Chapel Hill, 1959), 2: 594.

20. Merle Curti, *The Growth of American Thought* (New York, 1964), 107.

21. Stephen B. Weeks, *Church and State in North Carolina* (Baltimore, 1893), 61–62n. For strong feelings against non-Protestants in North Carolina, see the instructions to the county representatives at the Hillsborough Congress of August 1775. Protestant Christianity was to be "the religion of the State to the utter exclusion forever of all and every other (falsely so called) Religion, whether Pagan or Papal" (Elisha P. Douglass, *Rebels and Democrats* [Chapel Hill, 1955], 117).

22. Albert H. Smyth, ed., *The Writings of Benjamin Franklin* 10 vols. (New York, 1905–7), 9: 266–67.

23. J. Paul Selsam, *The Pennsylvania Constitution of 1776* (New York, 1971), 200, 217. For further opposition to the state constitution on grounds that the "Christian religion was not treated with proper respect," see Anne H. Wharton, "Thomas Wharton,

Jr., First Governor of Pennsylvania Under the Constitution," *The Pennsylvania Magazine of History and Biography* 5 (1881): 432–33.

24. Two decades earlier, when the Georgia legislature attempted to pass a "Bill for the Establishment of Religious Worship in this Province according to the Church of England," dissenters protested. One was a converted Jew, Joseph Ottolenghe. Another was John Martin Bolzius, minister of the Salzburgers, who reminded the legislature "that the province of Georgia was intended by His Majesty for an Asylum for all sorts of Protestants to enjoy full Liberty of Conscience" (Reba C. Strickland, *Religion and the State in Georgia in the Eighteenth Century* [New York, 1967], 103–4).

25. Charles R. Erdman, Jr., *The New Jersey Constitution of 1776* (Princeton, 1929), 54 n.

26. Robert J. Taylor, ed., *Massachusetts, Colony to Commonwealth: Documents on the Formation of Its Constitution, 1775–1780* (New York, 1972), 61, 155.

27. E. Francis Brown, *Joseph Hawley, Colonial Radical* (New York, 1931), 183.

28. L. F. Greene, ed., *The Writings of John Leland* (New York, 1969), 219–20. In a previous pamphlet (1791) Leland reminded his readers that the federal Constitution forbade "any religious test to qualify any officer in any department of federal government. Let a man be Pagan, Turk, Jew or Christian, he is eligible to any post in that government. So that if the principles of religious liberty . . . are supposed to be fraught with deism, fourteen states in the Union are now fraught with the same" (Ibid., 191–92).

29. Nathan Dane, *A General Abridgement and Digest of American Law*, 8 vols. (Boston, 1823–29), 2: 337.

30. Lynn W. Turner, *William Plumer of New Hampshire, 1759–1850* (Chapel Hill, 1962), 11.

31. Richard J. Purcell, *Connecticut in Transition: 1775–1818* (Middletown, 1963), 61. See also, Paul W. Coons, *The Achievement of Religious Liberty in Connecticut* (New Haven, 1936), 24.

32. Irving B. Richman, *Rhode Island: A Study in Separatism* (Boston, 1905), 181. The Rhode Island court cited an old law that stipulated "no person who does not follow the Christian religion can be admitted free of this colony" (ibid.).

33. The New York constitution required persons born outside the United States to take a naturalization oath renouncing all allegiance to "every foreign King, Prince, Potentate, and State, in all matters ecclesiastical as well as civil." John W. Pratt, in *Religion, Politics, and Diversity: The Church-State Theme in New York History* (Ithaca, 1967), 96–97, comments that "the animus against Catholicism apparent in the constitution seems to have been due less to any fear of Catholic worship than to the fear among eighteenth-century Protestants of papal influence." John Jay wished the restrictions against Catholics to be stronger.

34. Deists were regarded as a greater threat than Jews. William Duke, an Episcopalian clergyman and the author of *Observations on the Present State of Religion in Maryland*, defended the state constitution against the "artifice of Deists" who "sap the foundation of religious belief under the pretext of great good will, meaning only to clear away the rubbish of superstition" (cited in Thomas O'Brien Hanley, *The American Revolution and Religion: Maryland, 1770–1800* [Washington, D.C., 1971], 53). Duke might have had in mind William Vans Murray of Maryland, who was also an

Episcopalian but was steeped in the literature of rationalism. While a law student in England, he wrote six essays, *Political Sketches*, published in London in 1787 and reprinted in Philadelphia that same year. The final essay called for changes in the state constitutions of America to remove the bias against non-Christians (Alexander De-Conde, ed., "William Vans Murray on Freedom of Religion in the United States, 1787," *Maryland Historical Magazine* 50 [1955]: 282–90). But the bias was well rooted. In 1797 the vestry of Saint Peter's Church in Talbot County insisted that those who claimed to possess the religious qualifications for office be actually registered with a Christian congregation.

35. Charles F. James, *Documentary History of the Struggle for Religious Liberty in Virginia* (Lynchburg, 1900), 141.

36. Thomas E. Buckley, *Church and State in Revolutionary Virginia* (Charlottesville, 1977), 50–51.

37. Robert A. Rutland, ed., *The Papers of George Mason*, 3 vols. (Chapel Hill, 1970), 2:832.

38. Robert A. Rutland and William M. E. Rachal, eds., *The Papers of James Madison* (Chicago, 1973), 8:300.

39. Elizabeth Fleet, ed., "Madison's 'Detached Memoranda,'" *The William and Mary Quarterly* 3 (1946):556.

40. Paul L. Ford, ed., *The Writings of Thomas Jefferson*, 12 vols. (New York, 1904–5), 1:71. A nineteenth-century writer was critical of Jefferson's motives as author of the Virginia statute for religious freedom: "It gave its author great satisfaction, not because it embodied the principle of eternal justice, but because, by putting all religious sects on an equality, it seemed to degrade Christianity. . . . It was this that made the arch-infidel chuckle with satisfaction—not, we repeat, that the great principles imbodied in the measure were right" (Robert Baird, *Religion in America* [New York, 1856], 111). William W. Sweet, in *Religion in the Development of American Culture* (New York, 1952), 119, changes Baird's name to "Beard" and compliments his work as that of a "learned and accomplished Presbyterian."

41. Ford, *Jefferson*, 4:334.

42. Max Farrand, ed., *The Records of the Federal Convention* 4 vols. (New Haven, 1966), 3:227.

43. A sarcastic article in the *New Hampshire Spy*, 4 December 1787 (reprinted from the *Pennsylvania Gazette*) ridiculed a number of Anti-Federalist reasons for opposing ratification of the Constitution: because "a *Roman Catholic* and a *Jew* stood as good a chance of being president in the United States as a *Christian* or a *Protestant*," and because the Constitution took "no notice of the Sabbath"; did not provide for the "liberty of fishing and hunting, which were unalienable rights"; said "nothing in favor of American manufactures"; and had no provision "in favor of repairing our roads."

44. Jonathan Elliot, ed., *The Debates in the Several State Conventions on the Adoption of the Federal Constitution*, 5 vols. (Philadelphia, 1891), 2:148.

45. Collections of the Massachusetts Historical Society, 6th ser., 9 vols. (Boston, 1886–97), 4:389–90, 394.

46. Elliot, *Debates*, 4:199.

47. Morris Silverman, *Hartford Jews, 1659–1970* (Hartford, 1970), 108 n.

48. Kenyon, *Antifederalists*, lxix. Jackson T. Main, in *The Antifederalists: Critics*

of the Constitution, 1781–1788 (New York, 1974), 159, states that opponents of the Constitution, at least in New England, were "animated by desire to exclude non-Protestants from public office."

49. Henry F. May, in *The Enlightenment in America* (New York, 1976), 97, distinguishes between the Federalist authors of the Constitution, who were influenced by a "Moderate Enlightenment," a blend of rationalism and empiricism, and the Anti-Federalists, who were closer "to the radical Whig ideology with its radical Protestant overtones," and thus "sometimes attacked [the Constitution] for lacking a religious test." The evidence cited above blurs this distinction.

50. Elliot, *Debates*, 4:200. See also Louise I. Trenholme, *The Ratification of the Federal Constitution in North Carolina*, (New York, 1967), 178–80.

51. Morton Borden, ed., *The Antifederalist Papers* (East Lansing, 1965), 211.

52. Farrand, *Records*, 3:310.

53. Paul L. Ford, ed., *Pamphlets on the Constitution of the United States* (New York, 1888), 146.

54. Greene, *Leland*, 219–20. Leland asked, "Has not the world had enough proofs of the impolicy and cruelty of favoring a Jew more than a Pagan, Turk, or Christian; or a Christian more than either of them? Why should a man be proscribed, or any wife disgraced, for being a Jew, a Turk, a Pagan, or a Christian of any denomination, when his talents and veracity as a civilian entitles him to the confidence of the public?" (ibid., 223–24).

55. Stokes, *Church and State*, 1:314–18, 543.

56. Turner, *Plumer*, 47.

57. Nathaniel Bouton, ed., *Provincial Papers: Documents and Records Relating to the Province of New Hampshire*, 40 vols. (Concord, 1867–77), 10:58–62.

58. Jeremy Belknap, *The History of New Hampshire*, 2 vols. (New York, 1970), 2:245.

59. Stokes, *Church and State*, 1:534–36. See also, Edward F. Humphrey, *Nationalism and Religion in America, 1774–1789* (New York, 1965), 463–65.

60. Paul L. Ford, *Essays on the Constitution of the United States* (New York, 1892), 168–71.

61. William G. McLoughlin, *New England Dissent, 1630–1833: The Baptists and the Separation of Church and State*, 2 vols. (Cambridge, Mass., 1971), 2:989.

62. *The American Museum* 4 (1788):492–95.

63. Ibid.

64. Gaillard Hunt, ed., *The Writings of James Madison*, 9 vols. (New York, 1900–10), 5:271–72.

65. Madison stated in Congress that he "conceived this to be the most valuable amendment in the whole list" (*The Debates and Proceedings in the Congress of the United States*, 42 vols. [Washington, D.C., 1834–56], 1:783–84).

66. Russel B. Nye, *The Cultural Life of the New Nation, 1776–1830* (New York, 1963), 206.

67. See the marginal comments in the pamphlet *The Constitutions of the Several Independent States of America*, published by order of Congress (Philadelphia, 1781), owned by the Rosenbach Foundation. These comments deal with whether Jews can qualify for office in various states, depending upon how one interprets the meaning of

the word "Protestant." The comments have been ascribed to Gershom Seixas, *hazan* of Shearith Israel in New York, who fled to Philadelphia during the British occupation. One scholar vigorously denies the identification of Seixas as the author (see Jacob R. Marcus, "The Handsome Young Priest in the Black Gown," *Hebrew Union College Annual* 40 (1969–70): 16–17).

68. Schappes, *Documentary History*, 63–66, 583.

69. So did French Jews. They invoked the American Constitution in a petition in which they asked for equal rights, not merely toleration. A left-wing pamphleteer, De Laissac, responded in 1790 that religious freedom for Jews might be proper in America, which needed to augment its population, but not for France (see Arthur Hertzberg, *The French Enlightenment and the Jews* (New York, 1968), 347, 354).

70. Schappes, *Documentary History*, 77–84; Joseph L. Blau and Salo W. Baron, eds., *The Jews of the United States, 1790–1840: A Documentary History*, 3 vols. (New York, 1963), 1:8–11.

71. Louis Hartz, in "American Political Thought and the American Revolution," *American Political Science Review* 56 (1952):324, notes that Americans "refused to join in the great Enlightenment enterprise of shattering the Christian concept of sin."

72. B. F. Morris, *Christian Life and Character of the Civil Institutions of the United States* (Philadelphia, 1864), 443.

Chapter Two

1. Oscar Handlin, *Adventure in Freedom: Three Hundred Years of Jewish Life in America* (New York, 1954), 28.

2. Alfred D. Young, *The Democratic Republicans of New York* (Chapel Hill, 1967), 179, 185.

3. Eugene P. Link, *Democratic-Republican Societies, 1790–1800* (New York, 1942), 51.

4. George A. Lipsky, *John Quincy Adams: His Theory and Ideas* (New York, 1950), 122.

5. Federalist-Congregationalists were not the only ones to link Jews with Turks and infidels. The image was widespread and persistent. A letter to the editor of the *Alexandria*, Virginia, *Daily Advertiser*, 1 January 1806, complained that a visit of Indians to Congress forced females to give up their seats: "The ladies were compelled to quit the floor of the house, or to view the sight from the upper galleries amongst Turks, Jews, Infidels and Negroes, or to suspend their curiosity. As this is not one of the virtues of the fair sex they mounted amongst the dingy group." Fifty years later a Disciples of Christ minister, Jacob Creath, Jr., wrote in the *Christian Evangelist*: "The FILTHY practice of chewing tobacco and spitting on floors is bad enough for Jews and Turks, for negroes and rowdies, but it is worse in Christian men—still worse in Christian preachers—but worse of all, in Christian women" (David E. Harrell, Jr., *Quest for a Christian America* [Nashville, 1966], 184). A San Francisco woman wrote to the *Daily Alta California*, 24 December 1852, about the "peculiar but beautiful characteristic" of the United States, which gives "to all alien sects and creeds (alike to Heathen, Mahometan, Infidel and Jew) a liberty they possess in common in no other of

earth's dominions," but she cautioned that Americans should not "allow our own institutions to be invaded or perverted, and give [these] usurpers an advantage over our own rightful citizens." She admitted that "it may at first seem harsh to rank them [Jews] unconditionally with the others, but I am convinced that their influence in this city does more mischief than all the rest put together." In 1858 anti-Catholic reaction to the Mortara case confirmed Catholic suspicions that Jews were more acceptable to Protestants. A Catholic paper, the *New York Tablet*, stated it in rhyme: "A Turk, a Jew, or an Atheist / May enter here, but not a Papist" (Bertram W. Korn, *The American Reaction to the Mortara Case, 1858–1859* [Cincinnati, 1957], 138).

6. Morris U. Schappes, ed., *A Documentary History of the Jews in the United States* (New York, 1971), 92–96.

7. Morris U. Schappes, "Anti-Semitism and Reaction, 1795–1800," in *The Jewish Experience in America*, ed. Abraham J. Karp, 5 vols. (New York, 1969), 1:362–90.

8. Edwin Wolf and Maxwell Whiteman, *The History of the Jews of Philadelphia from Colonial Times to the Age of Jackson* (Philadelphia, 1956), 212–14.

9. Laura G. Pedder, ed., "The Letters of Joseph Dennie," *The Maine Bulletin* 38 (1936): 182.

10. Stephen E. Berk, in *Calvinism versus Democracy* (Hampden, Conn., 1974), 151, comments that "Congregational Federalists moved rapidly toward xenophobic nativism, as intruders threatened the status of the Puritan gentry." One should note, however, as does David H. Fischer, in *The Revolution of American Conservatism* (New York, 1965), 164–65, that Federalists in Philadelphia "showed signs that they had recognized the political dangers, if not the moral obliquities, of antisemitism. From 1806 onward, a Jew was usually on the most important Federalist electioneering committees in the City of Brotherly Love. Of course, in other parts of the country Federalists continued to capitalize upon antisemitism."

11. D. M'Allister, "Testimonies to the Religious Defect of the Constitution," *Proceedings of the National Convention to Secure the Religious Amendment of the Constitution of the United States, Held in Pittsburgh, February 4, 5, 1874* (Philadelphia, 1874), 41–45.

12. *Farmer's Weekly Museum*, 4 January 1803.

13. *The National Aegis*, 17 November 1802 (reprinted from the *United States Gazette*) and 15 December 1802; *Green Mountain Patriot*, 25 August 1802. See also, Jerry W. Knudson, "The Rage Around Tom Paine," *The New York Historical Society Quarterly* 53 (1969): 34–63.

14. Linda K. Kerber, *Federalists in Dissent* (Ithaca, 1970), 210.

15. *The Works of Daniel Webster*, 6 vols. (Boston, 1854), 6:153.

16. Lester J. Cappon, ed. *The Adams-Jefferson Letters*, 2 vols. (Chapel Hill, 1959), 2:512.

17. William G. McLoughlin, *New England Dissent 1630–1833: The Baptists and the Separation of Church and State*, 2 vols. (Cambridge, Mass., 2:1053.

18. Morris Silverman, *Hartford Jews 1659–1970* (Hartford, 1970), 6.

19. See the chapter entitled "Light on Early Connecticut Jewry," Jacob R. Marcus, *Studies in American Jewish History* (Cincinnati, 1969), 54–107.

20. Richard J. Purcell, *Connecticut in Transition: 1775–1818* (Middletown, 1963) 243.

21. Silverman, *Hartford Jews*, 7. The author adds, "And it was not until the new Constitution of 1965 was adopted that the phrases 'society or denomination of Christians' and 'Christian sect or mode of worship' were eliminated" (ibid.).

22. *Journal of Debates and Proceedings in the Convention of Delegates, Chosen to Revise the Constitution of Massachusetts* (Boston, 1853), 160–63.

23. Ibid., 170, 172–73, 205–7.

24. Ibid., 164–65, 171, 173–74. The Plumer quote is from his manuscript autobiography in the Library of Congress, 22 December 1820. It is worth noting that although political affiliation usually followed religious belief, in Austin's case the reverse was true. A staunch Republican, the scourge of Federalists, Austin later became a Whig. As such, serving as attorney general of Massachusetts, he joined other Whigs in defending Christian morality, becoming renowned for prosecuting Abner Kneeland for blasphemy.

25. Ibid., app., 632–33.

26. E. I. Devitt, ed., "Letters from the Archdiocesan Archives at Baltimore," *Records of the American Catholic Historical Society of Philadelphia*, 20 (1909): 275–76. See also Leo R. Ryan, *Old Saint Peter's* (New York, 1935), 84–85, and William H. Bennett, "Francis Cooper: New York's First Catholic Legislator," *Historical Records and Studies of the United States Catholic Historical Society*, 12 (1918): 29–38. One scholar comments that Albany "had a long tradition of tolerant pluralism," and that Protestants in 1798 gave money, and the city donated land, to build the first Catholic church in that city. William E. Rowley, "The Irish Aristocracy of Albany, 1798–1878," *New York History* 53 (1971): 278–79. Yet, four decades later, Jews and nativists in Albany actively cooperated against Catholics.

27. James T. Horton, *James Kent, A Study in Conservatism* (New York, 1939), 188–92. According to Horton, Kent "despised Popery; scorned the fanaticism of certain of the Protestant sects; and once, in the privacy of his club, had spoken of Christianity itself as a vulgar superstition from which cultivated men were free." Such double standards, between private beliefs and public expressions on religion, were common to both Federalist and Republican aristocrats. On the Ruggles case, see also Mark D. Howe, *The Garden and the Wilderness* (Chicago, 1965), 28–29.

28. *Reports of the Proceedings and Debates of the Convention of 1821, Assembled for the purpose of Amending the Constitution of the State of New York* (New York, 1970), 462–63. The sheriff Root referred to was Mordecai M. Noah. James Fenimore Cooper, in *Notions of the Americans*, 2 vols. (New York, 1963), 2:246, commented, "The sheriff of the city of New York, an officer elected by the people, was, a few years ago, a Jew! Now all the Jews in New York united, would not probably make three hundred voters. . . . Notwithstanding all this, the country is as much, or more, a Protestant and Christian country than any other nation on earth." Actually, Noah was appointed to the office of sheriff; when it later became an elective position Noah campaigned for it but was defeated.

29. Ibid., 466, 575, 577.

30. William Plumer, Manuscript Autobiography, Library of Congress, 14 February 1791 (emphasis added). The suggested punishment was more typical of seventeenth-century legislation in England and the colonies. "Fines, whippings, pillorying, prison, brandings, and banishment," one scholar notes, "were the common punishments.

Only Massachusetts actually imposed the death sentence for offenses against religion." In the eighteenth century there were "only about half a dozen convictions in all the colonies," the severest being meted out to "a sea captain in Maryland who blasphemed when scalding pitch burned his foot. He was fined twenty pounds, bored three times through the tongue, and imprisoned for a year" (Leonard W. Levy, *Treason against God: A History of the Offense of Blasphemy* (New York, 1981), 333–34).

31. Plumer, Manuscript, 2 February 1818.

32. McLoughlin, *New England Dissent*, 2:909.

33. Charles B. Kinney, *Church and State: The Struggle for Separation in New Hampshire, 1630–1900* (New York, 1955), 104.

34. Ibid., 131–32. Donald B. Cole, *Jacksonian Democracy in New Hampshire, 1800–1851* (Cambridge, Mass., 1970), 174, states that "Democratic pressure brought about this particular reform [abandonment of the test oath] at the Constitutional Convention of 1850." He fails to mention that the measure was defeated by the voters.

35. *Journal of the Constitutional Convention of the State of New Hampshire, December, 1876* (Concord, 1877), 32–33, 35–38, 40–41.

36. Kinney, *Church and State*, 134–44.

37. The final figures are taken from an unpaginated and undated pamphlet, *New Hampshire Anniversaries*, published by the state to celebrate its 300th anniversary of state government. Quite correctly it points out that "for many years up to 1968, the requirement that only Protestants could teach in public schools, had not, with general public approbation, been adhered to."

38. James H. Broussard, *The Southern Federalists, 1800–1816* (Baton Rouge, 1978), 65; and see 391–96 for an analysis of religion and party affiliation in the South.

39. Herbert T. Ezekiel and Gaston Lichtenstein, *History of the Jews of Richmond from 1769 to 1917* (Richmond, 1917), 127–28.

40. There is a substantial literature on the Maryland "Jew bill," including Benjamin Hartogensis, "Unequal Religious Rights in Maryland since 1776," *American Jewish Historical Society Publications* 25 (1917): 93–107; E. Milton Altfeld, *The Jew's Struggle for Religious and Civil Liberty in Maryland* (Baltimore, 1924); Joseph L. Blau, "The Maryland 'Jew Bill': A Footnote to Thomas Jefferson's Work for Freedom of Religion," *The Review of Religion* 8 (1944): 227–39; and Edward Eitches, "Maryland's 'Jew Bill,'" *American Jewish Historical Quarterly* 60 (1971): 258–79, which points out some faults of prior scholarship on this subject.

41. Altfeld, *Jew's Struggle*, 48–51, 80. See also, E. S. Thomas, *Reminiscences of the Last Sixty-Five Years*, 2 vols. (Hartford, 1840) 1:110–18; 2:92.

42. Ibid., 82; Joseph L. Blau and Salo W. Baron, *The Jews of the United States, 1790–1840, A Documentary History*, 3 vols. (New York, 1963), 1:40.

43. Ibid., 108–27; Blau, "Jew Bill," 230–32.

44. Blau and Baron, *Documentary History*, 1:44–47; Eitches, "Maryland's 'Jew Bill,'" 273.

45. Altfeld, *Jew's Struggle*, 26.

46. Eitches, "Maryland's 'Jew Bill,'" 266–67, 274; Wolf and Whiteman, *Jews of Philadelphia*, 370.

47. Blau and Baron, *Documentary History*, 1:48–49; Eitches, "Maryland's 'Jew Bill,'" 276.

48. Altfeld, *Jew's Struggle*, 32–33, 173–75.

49. Ibid., 44–45.

50. Ibid., 15; Blau, "Jew Bill," 237–39.

51. Schappes, *Documentary History*, 122–25; Blau and Baron, *Documentary History*, 1:27–32; *Raleigh Register*, 7 December 1809.

52. Leon Huhner, "The Struggle for Religious Liberty in North Carolina, with Special Reference to the Jews," *American Jewish Historical Society Publications* 16 (1907): 40–41, 48, 53–54.

53. Schappes, *Documentary History*, 122–25.

54. Huhner, "Struggle for Religious Liberty," 52, calls it "far-fetched"; but see Morton Borden and Harold Hyman, "Two Generations of Bayards Debate the Question: Are Congressmen Civil Officers?" *Delaware History* 6 (September 1953): 225–36.

55. Huhner, "Struggle for Religious Liberty," 52–55.

56. *Proceedings and Debates of the Convention of North Carolina* (Raleigh, 1836), 279–80.

57. Ibid., 246.

58. J. Herman Schauinger, *William Gaston, Carolinian* (Milwaukee, no date), 193. The debate is summarized on 188–98, and in Stephen B. Weeks, *Church and State in North Carolina* (Baltimore, 1893), 263–67.

59. For a summary and analysis of this speech, see Burton A. Konkle, *John Motley Morehead and the Development of North Carolina* (Spartanburg, 1971), 160–61.

60. *Proceedings and Debates*, 242, 254, 308, 328, 331.

61. Ibid., 311, 329, 394.

62. Harold J. Counihan, "The North Carolina Constitutional Convention of 1835: A Study in Jacksonian Democracy," *The North Carolina Historical Review* 46 (October 1969): 351–53.

63. Huhner, "Struggle for Religious Liberty," 63.

64. The address was republished in Leeser's *Discourses on the Jewish Religion* (Philadelphia, 1868), 86–88, to which he added an explanatory footnote stating that "the constitution of the state has been virtually so amended that Israelites are now citizens in full standing in North Carolina."

65. *The Occident*, November 1858.

66. Ibid., August 1860.

67. Ibid., March 1861.

68. J. G. de Roulhac Hamilton, ed., *The Papers of Thomas Ruffin*, 4 vols. (Raleigh, 1918), 2:92 n.

69. *Journal of the State Convention of the People of North Carolina* (Raleigh, 1862), 90–93; Huhner, "Struggle for Religious Liberty," 66–67. Leeser, in *The Occident*, July 1861, published a letter from M. I. Cohen of Baltimore reporting that he had heard from a friend in North Carolina that "our convention, now in session, have passed finally an ordinance removing the constitutional disability which existed against the Jews, and they have now the same civil rights as other citizens." The information obviously was erroneous.

70. The initial federal bill for "radical reconstruction" of the southern states required an oath "to be taken by citizens who wished to be qualified as members of the

constitutional convention . . . to be administered on the 'Holy Evangelist'—a form of oath to which no Israelite could conscientiously subscribe," the executive committee of the Board of Delegates of American Israelites reported. "Satisfied that this unjust discrimination entered into the proposed law simply by inadvertence, the Committee prepared a brief memorial, which was duly presented by Judge Kelly of Pennsylvania. The bill, as finally adopted by Congress, made no distinction, of a religious character, among citizens, and the form of the oath was modified so as not to be obnoxious to any" (*The Occident*, June 1867).

71. Niels H. Sonne, *Liberal Kentucky, 1780–1828* (New York, 1939), 6.

72. "The Provisional Constitution of Frankland," *The American Historical Magazine* 1 (1896): 48–63; John D. Barnhart, "The Tennessee Constitution of 1796: A Product of the Old West," *Journal of Southern History* 9 (1943): 532–48; Robert V. Remini, *Andrew Jackson and the Course of American Empire, 1767–1821* (New York, 1977), 77.

73. For a report of the legislative debate (over a Sunday trading bill for the counties of Santa Clara and Santa Cruz), which includes the remarks of Stow and others, see the *Sacramento Daily Union*, 17 March 1855; for the advertisement, ibid., 20 March 1855.

74. Colin B. Goodykoontz, "Some Controversial Questions Before the Colorado Constitutional Convention of 1876," *The Colorado Magazine* 17 (1940): 1–17.

75. Donald W. Hensel, "Religion and the Writing of the Colorado Constitution," *Church History* 30 (1961): 349–60.

76. *Denver Daily Tribune*, 14 January 1876.

Chapter Three

1. In Georgia the statutes provided that only judges or Christian ministers could perform legal marriage ceremonies. Jews were obliged to go through two services, that of a judge and of their own Rabbi. In the late 1840s, upon the petition of the Jews of Georgia, the state legislature altered the law to include Jewish ministers among those entitled to perform marriage ceremonies. Another statute, passed by Congress for the District of Columbia, permitted only Christian congregations to be incorporated. In 1856 Senator Lewis Cass presented the petition of "our Hebrew fellow-citizens of this District," adding his own endorsement that "such a distinction is an act of gross injustice, and, if continued after our attention is directed to it, it would be a disgrace to our jurisprudence." The bill for "the benefit of the Hebrew congregation in the City of Washington" passed both houses unanimously (*The Occident*, March and July 1856). An old Maryland law specified that the testimony of slaves or Indians could not be heard in a court of law in any case in which a Christian white person was concerned. Maryland passed "An Act relating to the law of Evidence" in 1847 removing that discrimination. (Thereafter slaves or Indians could not testify in a case involving any white, Jew or Christian.) The speaker of the Maryland house wrote to Dr. Joshua I. Cohen with pride: "That being *now* obliterated, our statute book is purged of an odious and offensive distinction, and now truly leaves, in the spirit of the constitution, and of the present age, every man the right to worship God according to

the dictates of his own conscience" (Ibid., April 1847). The speaker of the house was wrong, however. Leeser reported that there was one occupation—that of attorney— that required a Christian test oath and that requirement remained current until after the Civil War. In *The Occident*, September 1867, appears a notice that the new constitution of Maryland abolished the oath for attorneys, "and there is no legal or conscientious difficulty for Israelites to occupy any office." One should note, however, that Benjamin Hartogensis, in "Unequal Religious Rights in Maryland since 1776," 103, states (as of 1917) that each of Maryland's constitutions required a belief in God and in a hereafter: "Many deists, men of note, are unable to qualify as witnesses or jurors in Maryland today. The law also probably operates against such Jews as do not believe in bodily resurrection or in Paradise or Gehenna." A more recent scholar, Edward Eitches, "Maryland's 'Jew Bill,'" *American Jewish Historical Quarterly* 60 (1971): 278, points out that in Maryland "a Jew could not be legally married outside the church until 1927."

2. When James H. Hammond, governor of South Carolina, announced a day of "Thanksgiving, Humiliation, and Prayer" in 1844, he did so with the words "Whereas it becomes all Christian nations . . ." and exhorted "our citizens of all denominations to assemble at their respective places of worship, to offer up their devotions to God their Creator, and his Son Jesus Christ, the Redeemer of the world." The Jews of Charleston protested, charging Hammond "with such obvious *discrimination and preference* in the tenor of your proclamation, as amounted to an utter exclusion of a portion of the people of South Carolina." Hammond responded that "I have always thought it a settled matter that I lived in a Christian land! And that I was the temporary chief magistrate of a Christian people. That in such a country and among such a people I should be, publicly, called to an account, reprimanded and required to make amends for acknowledging Jesus Christ as the Redeemer of the world, I would not have believed possible, if it had not come to pass" (*The Occident*, January 1845). William F. Johnston, governor of Pennsylvania, issued a similar proclamation calling upon "all denominations of Christians" to "acknowledge their transgressions, supplicate through the merits of the Redeemer, the forgiveness of sins . . ." But Johnston, unlike Hammond, apologized immediately upon the receipt of numerous protests from Jewish citizens: "The terms of its composition . . . were not designated by me. . . . It was issued during my absence. . . . To the Israelites, among whom I have the honor to class many personal and political friends, I could mean no disrespect." The apology was printed on a handbill and distributed to voters in Philadelphia on election day, 10 October 1848 (ibid., November 1848). Many governors, once warned, were careful to phrase their proclamations in nonsectarian terms. Still, there continued to be numerous instances of Christian identifications, and Jews were alert to them. In 1850, Seabury Ford, governor of Ohio, thanked God for peace, health, harvests, and knowledge, "but especially for the Christian religion, for the inestimable blessings flowing to us from the prevalence of the principles of the 'everlasting gospel.'" The *Cincinnati Times* published the letter of A Jew who commented that Ford's proclamation "may do very well in a country where the State is the Church, but is unbecoming in a republican government, where all religions are equal, and is a positive impropriety against those good citizens of the State whose personal religious creed may be different to that of the occupant of the gubernatorial chair" (ibid., December 1850). During the Civil War,

Jews were concerned with weightier issues involving their rights to religious equality than Thanksgiving Day proclamations. In 1863, when the governor of Pennsylvania recommended that citizens "pray to God to give to Christian churches the grace to hate the thing which is evil," Isaac Leeser commented that he "deemed it useless to complain . . . as we had done so on several previous occasions only to find the offense again and again repeated" (ibid., January 1863).

3. Morris U. Schappes, *A Documentary History of the Jews in the United States* (New York, 1971), 252–63; see also, John A. Forman, "Lewis Charles Levin: Portrait of an American Demagogue," *American Jewish Archives* 12 (October, 1960): 150–94.

4. *The North American and United States Gazette*, 30 November 1864, reported on a Catholic "revival" service in Philadelphia: "The scene was such as Methodist protracted meetings often produce, but Catholic services very rarely. . . . Adults wept like children, and Protestant spectators who stood around were lost in wonder at what they never supposed could occur in a Romish sanctuary." See also, Jay P. Dolan, "American Catholics and Revival Religion, 1850–1900," *Horizons* 3 (1976): 39–57. To say that both groups were hostile to abolitionism does not mean there were not numerous individual exceptions. For Jews, see Jayme A. Sokolow, "Revolution and Reform: The Antebellum Jewish Abolitionists," *The Journal of Ethnic Studies* 9 (Spring, 1981): 27–41.

5. New York *Evening Post*, 24 February 1873.

6. Korn, *The American Reaction to the Mortara Case, 1858–1859* (Cincinnati, 1957), 36.

7. Ibid., 61, 82, 84. See also, by the same author, the chapter "The Know-Nothing Movement and the Jews," in Korn's *Eventful Years and Experiences: Studies in Nineteenth-Century American Jewish History* (Cincinnati, 1954).

8. Isaac M. Wise, *Reminiscences* (New York, 1945), 310–11.

9. Korn, *Mortara Case*, 25, 37–38, 100, 128.

10. Ibid., 48–49, 59–60, 68–70, 125.

11. James G. Heller, *Isaac M. Wise: His Life, Work, and Thought* (New York, 1965), 318–19. Wise's letter also protested government inaction on the Swiss treaty (see chapter 4).

12. Korn, *Mortara Case*, 88–89.

13. *The Occident*, March 1860.

14. Schappes, *Documentary History*, 632.

15. *The Occident*, September 1855.

16. D. M'Allister, "Testimonies to the Religious Defect of the Constitution," *Proceedings of the National Convention to Secure the Religious Amendment of the Constitution of the United States, Held in Pittsburgh, February 4, 5, 1874* (Philadelphia, 1874), 41.

17. The quotations of Austin, Taggart, and Lee are in ibid., 41–45. Morse's views are in William Gribbin, *The Churches Militant: The War of 1812 and American Religion* (New Haven, 1973), 34. The Reverend James Blythe, the leading Presbyterian clergyman in Kentucky and acting president of Transylvania University, delivered a sermon entitled "Our Sins Acknowledged" in 1815: "America is confessedly a Christian nation. She is considered such by all the nations of the earth. But where are the

records that substantiate the fact? . . . In which of our great national decrees, or national proclamations, or messages from our governors, is *God the Saviour* recognized? In none of them. With a solitary exception or two, any thing which has a religious bearing at all in these productions, is not characterized with aught that savors of Christianity. We could not have expected less from Plato or Cicero." An anonymous critic answered Blythe: "We would inform the reverend gentleman, that there are other religions beside the Christian, existing in this confederated republic; and if he knows no more about religion than politics, it may also be necessary to inform him, that there are Christians in the United States who do not agree with him as to the importance of recognizing *God the Saviour*". (Niels H. Sonne, *Liberal Kentucky, 1780–1828* (New York, 1939), 118–26.

18. M'Allister, "Testimonies," 47–48.

19. *The Duty of Christian Freemen to Elect Christian Rulers* (Philadelphia, 1828), 14. Ely stated, however, that "I do not wish any religious test to be prescribed by constitution and proposed to a man on his acceptance of any public trust. . . . Let it only be granted that Christians have the same rights and privileges in exercising the elective franchise which are accorded to Jews and Infidels" (ibid.).

20. D. X. Junkin, *The Oath: A Divine Ordinance, and an Element of the Social Constitution* (New York, 1845), 141.

21. B. F. Morris, *Christian Life and Character of the Civil Institutions of the United States* (Philadelphia, 1864), 760–62.

22. *The Occident*, February 1861. As an example, in 1818 a group of Covenanters from Randolph County, Illinois, petitioned the state constitutional convention to include a recognition that the scriptures were the "word of God and that the constitution is founded on the same." Their petition was ignored and, as a result, according to Governor Thomas Ford, they "refused to work the roads under the laws, serve on juries, hold any office, or do any other act showing that they recognized the government." Janet Cornelius, *A History of Constitution Making in Illinois* (Urbana, 1969), 23.

23. Isaac Leeser, *The Claims of the Jews to an Equality of Rights* (Philadelphia, 1841), 14.

24. *Reverses Needed: A Discourse delivered on the Sunday after the Disaster of Bull Run* (Hartford, 1861), 21, 23, 25–26.

25. M'Allister, "Testimonies," 53–54.

26. Ibid., 56–57.

27. Moses D. Hoge, *The Christian Statesman: A Discourse Delivered at the Funeral of Hon. John Hemphill* (Richmond, 1862), 12.

28. H. H. George, "Reminiscences," *The Christian Statesman*, November 1908.

29. *The Pittsburgh Dispatch*, 28–29 January 1864.

30. *The Occident*, January 1863.

31. Vallandigham said to Congress, "I move to strike out the words 'Christian denomination' in the seventh line, and in lieu thereof, to insert 'religious society.' I do it, Mr. Chairman, because there is a large body of men in this country, and one growing continually, of the Hebrew faith, whose rabbis and priests are men of great learning and unquestioned piety, and whose adherents are as good citizens and as true patriots as any in the country, but who are excluded by this section; and because, also, under

the Constitution of the United States, Congress is forbidden to make any law respecting the establishment of a State religion. While we are in one sense a Christian people, and yet in another sense not the most Christian people in the world, this is not a 'Christian *Government*', nor a Government which has any connection with any one form of religion in preference to any other form—I speak, of course, in a political sense alone. For these reasons I move the amendment." His amendment was rejected. Bertram Korn believes that a second, "perhaps more significant" reason for the rejection of Vallandigham's motion was anti-Catholic prejudice, because Congress had just turned down a prior amendment specifically authorizing brigadier generals to appoint Catholic chaplains "if there were no Catholic regimental chaplain in the brigade." Having refused "to authorize the appointment of Roman Catholic chaplains," Korn reasons, "they could not and would not add insult to injury by following with this approval of the commissioning of Rabbis as chaplains." Bertram W. Korn, "Congressman Clement L. Vallandigham's Championship of the Jewish Chaplaincy in the Civil War," *American Jewish Historical Quarterly* 53 [1963]: 188–91. The fact remains that Jews were excluded by the term "Christian denomination," while Catholics qualified.

32. Arthur B. Lapsley, ed., *The Writings of Abraham Lincoln*, 8 vols. (New York, 1906), 6:170–71.

33. Letter from B. Behrend, 4 December 1862, *The Occident*, January 1863.

34. Ibid., April 1864.

35. Stephen V. Ash, "Civil War Exodus: The Jews and Grant's General Orders No. 11," *The Historian* 44 (August 1982): 508–9.

36. John Y. Simon, ed., *The Papers of Ulysses S. Grant*, 10 vols. to date (Carbondale, 1967–), 5:238, 6:283, 394; 7:50. The fullest account is in Bertram W. Korn, *American Jewry and the Civil War* (Philadelphia, 1951).

37. An account of Rabbi Isaac Wise's visit to Washington is in Schappes, *Documentary History*, 473–76.

38. Simon, *Grant*, 7:55–56.

39. *The Occident*, March 1863; for an explanation of the circumstances in Paducah, see Ash, "Civil War Exodus," 513ff.

40. Ibid., February 1863.

41. Ibid., January 1869.

42. Lapsley, *Lincoln*, 6:253.

43. *Congressional Globe*, 37 Cong., 3 sess., 1448, 1501.

44. Lapsley, *Lincoln*, 6:270–72. See also, William J. Wolff, *The Almost Chosen People: A Study of the Religion of Abraham Lincoln* (New York, 1959), 162–64.

45. Letters of endorsement were read at each meeting. See *The Pittsburgh Dispatch*, 28 January 1864 and *The Philadelphia Inquirer*, 7 July and 1 December 1864. At the November 1864 Philadelphia convention, following the address of Judge William Strong, the Reverend Kingston Goddard (an Episcopalian) spoke to the assembly: "He considered that now, when our armies were victorious, and when we are expecting to hear almost daily that the rebellion is crushed, it would be a very proper time to acknowledge the hand of God in our government" (*Public Ledger*, 30 November 1864).

46. Edward L. Pierce, *Memoirs and Letters of Charles Sumner*, 4 vols. (Boston, 1877–93), 4:174.

47. *North American and United States Gazette*, 1 December 1864. The *New York Times* took a position against the movement in an editorial on 2 February 1864.

48. *The Occident*, August 1863.

49. Ibid., February 1865.

50. Ibid.

51. Ibid.

52. Pierce, *Sumner*, 4:175.

53. *North American and United States Gazette*, 9 July 1864.

54. T. P. Stevenson, "Origin and Progress of the Movement to Secure the Religious Amendment of the Constitution of the United States," *Proceedings of the National Convention to Secure the Religious Amendment of the Constitution of the United States, Held in Cincinnati, January 31 and February 1, 1872* (Philadelphia, 1872), viii–x.

55. Ibid.

56. *The Occident*, August 1867.

57. Ibid., July 1868.

58. *Congressional Globe*, 40 Cong., 3 sess., 1028, 1032, 1035, 1037.

59. *The Christian Statesman*, 1 April 1870, and republished in the same journal in March 1938 on the seventy-fifth anniversary of the National Reform Association.

60. See the editorials and letters in *The Monmouth Atlas* of Warren County, Illinois, 10 February and 3 March 1871. A typical letter is by D. S. F.: "But in the Constitution of the United States, God and His law, and His Son, by whom He administers His law, are not once mentioned. This is a grievous defect, as it puts God out of the view of the political actors, and makes them consider no accountability higher than their constituents. . . . There is an irresistible temptation to practice fraud and deal in scandalous corruption. Facts from all parts of the country illustrate these statements. The corruption of the ballot, gross revenue frauds, and outrageous legislation, whereof the motive proceeds from the lobby in the shape of corrupting bribes. . . . These evils increase daily." Two years later the New York *Tribune*, 1 March 1873, took particular delight in pointing out "the fact that nearly if not quite all the incriminating parties"— Vice President Colfax; Senators Patterson of New Hampshire, Harlan of Iowa, and Pomeroy of Kansas—were "of the class which has of late come to be known, in distinction from the average bad politician, as 'Christian Statesmen.'"

61. W. H. Littlejohn, *The Constitutional Amendment: Or, The Sunday, The Sabbath, The Change, and Restitution* (Battle Creek, 1873), iii, 83.

62. Samuel T. Spear, *Religion and the State* (New York, 1876), 223. The volume is a collection of articles that appeared originally in *The Independent*. From Paris, the author, William A. Scott, wrote to his friend Henry H. Haight, governor of California, on 10 April 1868: "I am altogether opposed to the present rage for tinkering with our Constitution or adding any religious clauses to it. . . . It is exceedingly strange that as the old world is struggling out of the tyranny and corruption of an alliance of the Church with the State, we should be struggling to set the same yoke upon our necks" (Henry R. Huntington Library, San Marino, California).

63. New York *Herald*, 23, 27, 28 February 1873. The writer of this editorial is unknown, but it represents a substantial change in policy from an earlier period when James G. Bennett, a Catholic, used the *Herald* to attack Jews. He especially disliked

Mordecai Noah and delighted in using epithets such as "Shylock," "base Judean," "old clothes Jew," et cetera. Jews, wrote Bennett, were "a race of secret conspirators against [the Christian] religion . . . without a single redeeming feature." In 1850 Bennett accused Jews of practicing ritual murder. Jonathan D. Sarna, *Jacksonian Jew: The Two Worlds of Mordecai Noah* (New York, 1981), 119–20.

64. *Christian Advocate*, 6 March 1873.

65. Dennis L. Pettibone, "Caesar's Sabbath: The Sunday-Law Controversy in the United States, 1879–1892," (Ph.D. diss., University of California, Riverside, 1979), 59, 88.

66. William Parsons, "Christianizing a State," *The Christian Statesman*, July 1913. See also, the testimony of T. P. Stevenson before the judiciary subcommittee of the House of Representatives in ibid., June 1910.

67. Isaac A. Cornelison, *The Relation of Religion to Civil Government in the United States of America* (New York, 1895), 237. Elizabeth Cady Stanton also opposed the Christian amendment. In 1888 she spoke out against the movement in her "Address of Welcome to the International Council of Women." Ellen C. DuBois, ed., *Elizabeth Cady Stanton and Susan B. Anthony: Correspondence, Writings, Speeches* (New York, 1981), 86, 208–15.

68. *The Christian Statesman*, November 1912.

69. Ella M. George, "Brief History of Birth of the National Reform Association," ibid., December 1933.

70. Marty, *The Righteous Empire: The Protestant Experience in America* (New York, 1970), 249.

71. Quoted by J. M. W., "Political Preparation for the Christian Amendment," *The Christian Statesman*, August 1912. The author comments that Greeley's words were "crude" and did not have "any possible relation to the adoption of a provision in our constitutional law which would give direction to the nation in the moral crises which arise in our political life." R. C. Wylie, in "Sesqui-centennial Papers," ibid., July-August 1926, quoted another statement of Greeley's (to which he took exception): "We deny that this is a Christian nation. France, Spain, Russia, Austria, Mexico, Portugal, Brazil, etc., are Christian nations, no matter how many of their people may be non-Christians; this country is *not* Christian, though a majority of its inhabitants probably are. Almighty God is *not* the source of authority and power in our government; the people of the United States are such source."

Chapter Four

1. Lester J. Cappon, Jr., *The Adams-Jefferson Letters*, 2 vols. (Chapel Hill, 1959), 2:496.

2. Arthur Schlesinger, Jr., *The Age of Jackson* (Boston, 1953), 352–53.

3. Robert T. Handy, *A Christian America: Protestant Hopes and Historical Realities* (New York, 1971), 56.

4. *The Christian Statesman*, April 1932 (emphasis added).

5. William A. Blakely, ed., *American State Papers Bearing on Sunday Legislation* (New York, 1970), 163 n.

6. Ibid., 99 n.

7. *The Christian Statesman*, April 1932.

8. Hunter Miller, ed., *Treaties and Other International Acts of the United States of America*, 8 vols. (Washington, D.C., 1931–48), 2:371.

9. Charles B. Todd, *Life and Letters of Joel Barlow* (New York, 1886), 86, 90 n., 161.

10. Oscar Straus, *Under Four Administrations* (New York, 1922), 143–46.

11. Sherman D. Wakefield, "The Treaty with Tripoli of 1796–97," *Progressive World* (1955): 27–30.

12. The episode of Noah's dismissal is covered in an older biography by Isaac Goldberg, *Major Noah: American-Jewish Pioneer* (Philadelphia, 1936), and a recent (and far superior) one, Jonathan D. Sarna, *Jacksonian Jews: The Two Worlds of Mordecai Noah* (New York, 1981). See also, Robert Gordis, "Mordecai M. Noah: A Centenary Evaluation," *Publications of the American Jewish Historical Society* (1951), 41:7. Noah disagreed with Leeser on the question of the wisdom or necessity of Article 11. Decades later he wrote in the New York *Commercial Advertiser* that "Mr. Barlow was a free-thinker in religious matters, and I disapproved of the article, because it was engrafting his private prejudices upon a solemn contract made with a foreign nation, when the object contemplated could have been reached without using any language calculated to offend the religious attachments of the people, and when, at all events, it was quite unnecessary to inform the Mussulmans of Tripoli that in effect we had no religion at all." Leeser reprinted this statement and responded in *The Occident*, February 1850: "All the words mean to convey is, that Christianity does, as such, not enter into the polity of the government; and that the constitution, the fundamental law, has no necessary connection with either the dogmas or precepts of Christianity. The proposition, we always thought, was so evident, that we could not help wondering, and our astonishment is not lessened at this day, that people should even dare to call this a Christian country and speak of the population as a Christian people."

13. Miller, *Treaties*, 7:804.

14. For much of the correspondence, see Senate Executive Document No. 30, 36 Cong., 1st sess., U.S. Serial No. 1032.

15. *Journal of the Executive Proceedings of the Senate*, 11:19.

16. *The Occident*, September 1859.

17. W. A. P. Martin, *A Cycle of Cathay* (New York, 1896), 181–84. Reed was congratulated in the press. See, for example, the *Los Angeles Star*, 2 October 1858, which cited the commercial advantages and the fact that "Christianity is to be tolerated throughout the Empire."

18. Hosea B. Morse, *The International Relations of the Chinese Empire*, 3 vols. (London, 1910), 1:332.

19. Tyler Dennett, *Americans in Eastern Asia* (New York, 1941), 563.

20. Frederick W. Williams, ed., "The Journal of S. Wells Williams," *Journal of the North-China Branch of the Royal Asiatic Society* (1911), 42:86, 89.

21. Michael Pollak, *Mandarins, Jews, and Missionaries* (Philadelphia, 1980), 115.

22. Martin, *Cathay*, 273–79. See also, Pollak, *Mandarins*, 164–71, for a full account of Martin's visit and his purposes. Writes Pollak, "He was, after all, a missionary, and the people to whom he was addressing his plea would have had to be excep-

tionally naive to believe that he honestly wanted the members of the Kaifeng *kehillah* to become sincere and pious Jews again. The truth was, of course, that he wanted nothing of the sort. He had, in fact, already candidly defined his true objective—the Christianization of the *kehillah*—in a letter . . . to a colleague."

23. *The Occident*, June 1853 and January 1854. Pollak, *Mandarins*, pp. 171ff., contains an account of the deep concern and the flurry of activities of various Jews and Jewish organizations in the United States and in Britain in behalf of Chinese Jews. These activities—fund-raising, dispatching representatives—had few practical results. The fact remains, as Leeser noted, that most western Jews had little sense of common religious identification with oriental Jews and were not interested in the subject except as a curiosity.

24. *The Occident*, September 1859. Leeser was under the mistaken impression that the treaty with Japan that was negotiated by Townsend Harris, like that with China, "while especially providing for American citizens professing the Christian belief, protection for their worship, makes no similar provision for the professors of Judaism." The treaty with Japan made no religious distinctions.

25. Dennett, *Eastern Asia*, p. 415.

26. Miller, *Treaties*, 5:859–60.

27. Ibid., 5:863.

28. Ibid., 5:878–79. Rabbi Isaac M. Wise was indignant over the Swiss treaty, as his editorials in *The Israelite* indicate. But he was completely taken in by Webster. In his *Reminiscences*, (New York, 1945), 184–86, he tells of a four-way conversation with Webster, Senator Judah P. Benjamin, and Lieutenant Matthew Maury, a well-known scholar. Webster introduced Wise to Benjamin: "Mr. Senator, my friend [Wise] is of your race. I would have said your co-religionist, but I do not know how much or how little you believe; and in truth we four are all co-religionists, since we are all Unitarians." Maury objected, stating that he did not belong to any church organization. So did Benjamin, stating that Judaism and Unitarianism were entirely different. Wise fails to say what his response was, but he goes on to call Webster "the greatest intellect of whom America could boast." Obviously Wise did not realize that Webster had been widely acclaimed by Protestant ministers some years earlier for "demonstrating [in his argument in the Vidal case] the vital importance of Christianity to the success of our free institutions"; or that Webster initially saw nothing wrong with the Swiss treaty. There is, however, some controversy over the accuracy of Wise's recollection of this conversation. James G. Heller, *Isaac M. Wise, His Life, Work and Thought* (New York, 1965), 723–24.

29. Sol M. Stroock, "Switzerland and American Jews," reprinted in *The Jewish Experience in America*, ed. Abraham J. Karp, 5 vols. (New York, 1969), 3:80.

30. *The Occident*, March 1851.

31. *Journal of the Executive Proceedings of the Senate*, 8:290.

32. Miller, *Treaties*, 5:846 (emphasis added).

33. Ibid., 5:886–87 (emphasis added).

34. Ibid., 5:880.

35. Stroock, "Switzerland," 93.

36. Cyrus Adler and Aaron M. Margalith, *American Intercession on Behalf of Jews in the Diplomatic Correspondence of the United States* (New York, 1943), 300–301.

37. Stroock, "Switzerland," 86.

38. *The Occident*, May 1854.

39. Stroock, "Switzerland," 87; Samuel Rezneck, "The Strange Role of a Jewish Sea Captain in the Confederate South," *American Jewish History* (September 1978), 68:64–73. During the Civil War his brother Uriah Levy remained loyal to the Union, and Jonas Levy took the Confederate side.

40. Stroock, "Switzerland," 83–84.

41. Ibid.

42. Ray A. Billington, *The Protestant Crusade, 1800–1860* (New York, 1938), 267–68.

43. Lawrence Kehoe, ed., *Complete Works of the Most Rev. John Hughes*, 2 vols. (New York, 1865), 2:486.

44. W. L. G. Smith, *The Life and Times of Lewis Cass* (New York, 1856), 585–86.

45. *Congressional Globe*, 33 Cong. 1st sess., 1187.

46. Kehoe, *Hughes*, 2:465, 476–83.

47. *Congressional Globe*, 33 Cong., 1st sess., 681–91.

48. *The Occident*, May 1854.

49. Ibid., September 1857.

50. Stroock, "Switzerland," 96–97.

50. *The Occident*, December 1857.

51. Ibid.

52. Stroock, "Switzerland," 97–99.

53. Ibid., 103–4.

54. *Congressional Globe*, 35 Cong., 2d sess., 1600–1601; 36 Cong., 1st sess., 1359.

55. Adler and Margalith, *American Intercession*, 311, 313, 317.

56. *The Occident*, September, October, November, and December 1861.

57. The resolution referred to conflicting interpretations of the United States-Russian Treaty of 1832. See Carl G. Winter, "The Influence of the Russo-American Treaty of 1832 on the Rights of American Jewish Citizens," *Publications of the American Jewish Historical Society* (1951), 41:163–94.

58. *Congressional Record*, 52 Cong., 1 sess., 5228.

59. *The American Jewish Year Book, 5669* (Philadelphia, 1908), 249.

60. Ibid., 249–50.

61. See Albert M. Friedenberg, "The Jews and the American Sunday Laws," *Publications of the American Jewish Historical Society* (1903), 11:114–15; John Samuel, "Some Cases in Pennsylvania Wherein Rights Claimed by Jews are Affected," in ibid., (1897), 5:36. See also, Max Kohler, "The Doctrine that 'Christianity is a Part of the Common Law,' and Its Recent Judicial Overthrow in England, with particular reference to Jewish Rights," in ibid., (1928), 31:126 n.

Chapter Five

1. Alexis de Tocqueville, *Democracy in America* (New York, 1969), 293.
2. James Bryce, *The American Commonwealth*, 2 vols. (London, 1889), 2:560–61. Henry S. Commager, *The American Mind* (New Haven, 1950), 163, concludes that "in everything but law, America, at the opening of the twentieth century, was a Christian nation." Sidney E. Mead, *The Nation with the Soul of a Church* (New York, 1975), 19, notes: "The United States was never Protestant in the sense that its constitutional and legal structure was rooted in or legitimized by particularistic Protestant theology." That is true, but numerous laws and judicial decisions did reflect the will of the Protestant majority.
3. Theodore Schroeder, *Constitutional Free Speech Defined and Defended* (New York, 1919), 122–23.
4. Jay also stated that "infidels and Christians, and politicians of every name and character, have an equal and undoubted right to publish their sentiments, and to endeavor to make converts to them." These views were exceptional, running counter to Jay's political association (Federalist) and his religious background. As a young man he wrote two prize essays on the topic "Sunday: Its Value as a Civil Institution and Its Sacred Character." He was trained by Timothy Dwight at Yale—where he participated in debates with topics such as: "Ought infidels to be excluded from office? Ought religion to be supported by law?" He played an important part in founding the American Bible Society. Bayard Tuckerman, *William Jay and the Constitutional Movement for the Abolition of Slavery* (New York, 1969), iv, 7, 10–13. Jay's charge to the grand jury was later cited by the defense in the Abner Kneeland blasphemy prosecution.
5. Robert Richardson, *Memoirs of Alexander Campbell*, 2 vols. (Cincinnati, 1913), 2:534.
6. 5 Bin. R., 562–63.
7. 11 S & R., 395ff.
8. From the *Christian Chronicle*, reprinted in *The Occident*, June 1849.
9. Henry S. Commager, "The Blasphemy of Abner Kneeland," *The New England Quarterly* 8 (March, 1935): 34–35; Leonard W. Levy, "Satan's Last Apostle in Massachusetts," *American Quarterly* 5 (Spring, 1953): 19, 23.
10. Lester J. Cappon, *The Adams-Jefferson Letters*, 2 vols. (Chapel Hill, 1959), 2:422.
11. Ibid., 2:607–8.
12. William W. Story, ed., *Life and Letters of Joseph Story*, 2 vols. (Freeport, New York, 1971), 2:8–9.
13. Joseph Story, *Commentaries on the Constitution of the United States*, 3 vols. (New York, 1970), 3:705, 723. On the testimony of non-Christians in a court of law, see Frank Swancara, *Obstruction of Justice by Religion* (New York, 1971), 27–60.
14. Story, *Life and Letters*, 2:473.
15. 15 US 84–87.
16. Timothy Dwight, *Travels in New England and in New York*, 4 vols. (Cambridge, Mass., 1969), 3:234; 4:70, 255.
17. de Tocqueville, *Democracy*, 714.

18. In Maryland the fine was $3.33, which in one case was levied against two Jews in Baltimore who were arrested, although they worked privately within their own house on Sunday. Isaac Leeser, *The Claims of the Jews to an Equality of Rights* (Philadelphia, 1841), 90 n.

19. Richardson, *Campbell*, 2:529–30. Ross was a Federalist. His opposition was not to Sunday laws, but to vigilante tactics. On "moral societies" in Connecticut, see Stephen E. Berk, *Calvinism versus Democracy* (Hampden, Conn., 1974), 186–87.

20. Paul E. Johnson, *A Shopkeepers Millenium: Society and Revivals in Rochester, New York, 1815–1837* (New York, 1978), 84–88.

21. Walter Lowrie and Walter S. Franklin, eds., *American State Papers. Class VII: Post Office Department* (Washington, 1834), 232–33, 236–37.

22. Ibid., 238–41, 261–64.

23. William A. Blakely, ed., *American State Papers Bearing on Sunday Legislation* (New York, 1970), 254.

24. Robert T. Handy, *A Christian America: Protestant Hopes and Historical Realities* (New York, 1971), 48.

25. Many Lutherans were reluctant to speak out for stronger Sunday laws because of the large immigration of German members of their church in the 1840s and 1850s. These immigrants carried with them the anti-Semitism of their homeland and were, says one scholar, "more prone to view the presence of Jews as a threat to their aspirations than were native-born Americans." Robert A. Rockaway, "Anti-Semitism in an American City: Detroit, 1850–1914," *American Jewish Historical Quarterly* 64 (September 1974): 43.

26. See, for example, John F. Reynolds, "Piety and Politics: Evangelism in the Michigan Legislature, 1837–1860," *Michigan History* 61 (Winter 1977): 327–29.

27. Blakely, *American State Papers*, 328–40.

28. Louis Ruchames and Walter M. Merrill, eds., *The Letters of William Lloyd Garrison*, 6 vols. (Cambridge, Mass., 1971–81), 2:178–79, 247, 281, 316, 320; 4:160, 493, 595; 6:429.

29. Salo W. Baron, *Steeled by Adversity: Essays and Addresses on American Jewish Life* (Philadelphia, 1971), 103.

30. Charles F. Adams, ed., *Memoirs of John Quincy Adams*, 12 vols. (Philadelphia, 1874–77), 12:110–13.

31. Blakely, *American State Papers*, p. 360. Adams's poem, "Sabbath Morning," contains these lines: ". . . in orison sublime / Souls to the throne of God ascend / Let no unhallowed child of time / Profane pollutions with them blend." John Q. Adams, *Poems of Religion and Society* (Auburn, New York, 1850), 56.

32. Morris U. Schappes, *A Documentary History of the Jews in the United States* (New York, 1971), 279–81. Jonathan D. Sarna, in *Jacksonian Jew: The Two Worlds of Mordecai Noah* (New York, 1981), 134, comments: "Noah . . . felt that for the sake of a national consensus, Jews and others who considered the seventh day of the week as holy should resignedly agree to assume the burdens which two days of rest necessarily entailed. . . . If police regulations happened to stamp Protestant practice with the seal of law, that was perfectly legal; majority ruled. Isaac Leeser and others, alarmed at growing neglect of the Jewish sabbath, disagreed. They sided with liberals

who termed Sunday laws religious coercion. To Noah this was heresy. He lectured his fellow Jews on the impropriety of even raising such an issue in debate."

33. Kerry M. Olitzky, "The Sunday-Sabbath Movement in American Reform Judaism: Strategy or Evolution?" *American Jewish Archives* 34 (April, 1982): 77–78.

34. *The Occident*, July 1847. Leeser noted that "one of the principal reasons why so many violate the Sabbath, *when if left to their own convictions they would be pious Jews*, is that they fear their gentile neighbors." See the letter of S. M. Isaacs on Jews violating the Sabbath in ibid., February 1845.

35. Richard C. Wylie, *Sabbath Laws in the United States* (Pittsburgh, 1905), 25; Joseph L. Blau and Salo W. Baron, eds., *The Jews of the United States, 1790–1840: A Documentary History*, 3 vols. (New York, 1963), 1:24–26.

36. *The Occident*, March 1847.

37. Ibid.

38. Ibid., March 1848. The tribunal was the court of errors, which, wrote Leeser, consisted "of all the Law Judges and the Chancellors."

39. Ibid., April 1848.

40. Ibid., July 1848.

41. Ibid., September 1848.

42. Schappes, *Documentary History*, 279–81.

43. *The Occident*, April 1848.

44. 1 Penr. & W., 12–13.

45. Reprinted in *The Occident*, June 1849.

46. Ibid.

47. Ibid., May, June, July, and August 1854, for the entire decision.

48. Ibid., August 1855.

49. Ibid., October 1859.

50. Ibid.

51. Wylie, *Sabbath Laws*, 77–78.

52. Herbert T. Ezekiel and Gaston Lichtenstein, *The History of the Jews of Richmond from 1769 to 1917* (Richmond, 1917), 110.

53. Ibid., pp. 104–8.

54. *The Occident*, September 1846.

55. Ezekiel and Lichtenstein, *Jews of Richmond*, 112–15.

56. *The Occident*, December 1849.

57. Jefferson and Madison had endorsed a "Bill for Punishing Disturbers of Religious Worship and Sabbath Breakers" in Virginia, which was passed in 1786, at the same time as the famous statute on religious liberty. Virginians believed, writes one author, "apparently, that orthodox Christianity deserved at least that small measure of tranquilizing sustenance from the state" (Mark D. Howe, *The Garden and the Wilderness* [Chicago, 1965], 96–97). See also, Wilber G. Katz, *Religion and American Constitutions* (Evanston, 1964), 15. Not too much should be made of this fact, however. Jefferson and Madison also endorsed a "Bill for Appointing Days of Public Fasting and Thanksgiving" by the governor. But as successive presidents they resisted religious pressures to issue such proclamations. "I do not believe," wrote Jefferson in 1808, "it is for the interest of religion to invite the civil magistrate to direct its exer-

cises, its discipline, or its doctrines." Moreover: "Fasting and prayer are religious exercises. The enjoining them an act of discipline. Every religious society has a right to determine for itself the *times* of these exercises, and the objects proper for them, according to their own particular tenets; and this right can never be safer than in their own hands, where the constitution has deposited it" (Paul L. Ford, *The Writings of Thomas Jefferson*, 12 vols. [New York, 1904–5], 11:7–8, (emphasis added). Jefferson was speaking of the federal government, but there is little doubt that neither he nor Madison approved of judges sustaining the constitutionality of Sunday laws on the basis of the common law or by declaring the United States to be a Christian nation.

58. *The Occident*, March 1850.

59. Ibid., September 1858. Three decades later twenty-two states had Sunday laws with exemptions of some kind for Saturday-keepers, fourteen did not; and the issue was more hotly debated than ever before. National Reform Association leaders joined other Christian groups in an effort to do away with all exemptions, maintaining that Jews, "the strangers within our gates," must yield to the will of the Christian majority. Many Jews were ready to do that by changing their day of worship to Sunday. Others were content to accept Sunday laws with exemptions. But some Jews, Seventh-Day Baptists, and Seventh-Day Adventists in effect adopted Leeser's position that all such laws were religious in nature and were unconstitutional. See Dennis L. Pettibone, "Caesar's Sabbath, The Sunday-Law Controversy in the United States, 1879–1892" (Ph.D. diss., University of California, Riverside, 1979), 330–38.

60. Hinton R. Helper, *The Land of Gold: Reality versus Fiction* (Baltimore, 1855), 109. Helper dedicated this book to John Motley Morehead of North Carolina. See also, Robert E. Levinson, *The Jews in the California Gold Rush* (New York, 1978).

61. E. S. Capron, *History of California* (Boston, 1854), 156.

62. Horace Bushnell, *Society and Religion: A Sermon for California*, delivered at the First Congregational Church of San Francisco, 6 July 1856. Pamphlet in Special Collections, University of California, Santa Barbara, 18, 23–24.

63. See, for example, the *Daily Alta California*, 5 June 1858, on how lexicographers define the meaning of "tavern."

64. *Sacramento Daily Union*, 22 June 1858.

65. Albert M. Friedenberg, "Solomon Heydenfeldt: A Jewish Jurist of Alabama and California," *Publications of the American Jewish Historical Society* 10 (1902): 129–40.

66. Terry's opinion is reprinted in *The Occident*, September 1858.

67. Ibid.

68. For Field's early religious training and his dissent in the Newman case, see Carl B. Swisher, *Stephen J. Field* (Washington, 1930), 5–16, 77–82.

69. Field's dissent was reprinted in *The Occident*, September 1858. It became, as Felix Frankfurter noted in the case of *McGowan v. Maryland* (366 US 459–543), "a leading pronouncement on the constitutionality of Sunday laws." That is so. It became a leading pronouncement, however, not because Field said anything previous judges had not, but because of the novelty of the majority decision, the attention it received, and thus the attention directed to Field's rebuttal. In the McGowan case William O. Douglas, dissenting, praised Terry's opinion as having "accurately summarized" the history and constitutional issues of Sunday laws a century earlier.

70. Wylie, *Sabbath Laws*, 7, 130, 152, 155.

71. 143 US 471.

72. David J. Brewer, *The United States a Christian Nation* (Philadelphia, 1905), 29–30, 58.

73. Anson P. Stokes, *Church and State in the United States* 3 vols. (New York, 1950), 1:879–81; Baron, *Steeled by Adversity*, 327.

74. Blakely, *American State Papers*, 370–77; *Congressional Record*, 25–26 May and 11 July 1892, 4693, 4716, 5993-6004. For a full account of the groups favoring and opposing this legislation, see Pettibone, "Caesar's Sabbath," 256–78.

75. Olitzky, "The Sunday-Sabbath Movement," 80.

BIBLIOGRAPHICAL NOTE

W. Melvin Adams, an official of the General Conference of Seventh-Day Adventists, stated in 1979 that "the free exercise of religion proclaimed by the Constitution has become an empty promise to many people in the United States. Its absence has been accepted by many to be their price for marching to the beat of a different drummer. A strange paradox has arisen in our country. It says that you may have your freedoms as long as you are in the majority or as long as you are in the mainstream. But if your beliefs are different, you may believe them but you may not practice them unless they do not conflict with the majority, or unless they do not conflict with the wishes of an employer, or unless they are not inconvenient."

Most Jews today would not subscribe to that opinion, and it is questionable if a majority of Jews would have in the nineteenth century. But Isaac Leeser said precisely the same thing. No other Jewish leader worked quite as hard or as consistently to achieve the goal of legal and constitutional equality for all. This is why this study concentrates upon *The Occident*, rather than upon the journals of his coreligionists and sometimes competitors, Isaac M. Wise's *The Israelite*, Robert Lyon's *The Asmonean*, and Stanley M. Isaac's *The Jewish Messenger*.

This study dissents from a common view, best expressed by Salo W. Baron in *Steeled by Adversity: Essays and Addresses on American Jewish Life* (Philadelphia, 1971), 28, that "Jews were, as a rule, incorporated in the American body politic, so to say, in complete absent-mindedness. The very emancipation, established as a matter of general principle, through the federal and states' constitutions, was achieved with practically no reference to Jews as such." Jews were present, mainly in the myths—how could they not be?—but also in the flesh. In either case, although the Protestant majority had greater fears, it was rare indeed for Jews not to be included in their catalog of potential evils. That is apparent from the debates in various state constitutional conventions well into the nineteenth century.

Moses Rischin has commented that for "the first five decades of the American republic" the sources on Jews are "painfully thin" and "infuriatingly anonymous." Nevertheless, what is available reveals a great deal of Jewish perceptions and how Jews were perceived. There are two excellent collections of primary sources: Morris U. Schappes (ed.), *A Documentary History of the Jews in the United States, 1654–1875* (New York, 1971), a work of extraordinary scholarship despite the critical remarks of Baron in *Steeled by Adversity* (74–79); and Joseph L. Blau and Salo W. Baron (eds.), *The Jews of the United States, 1790–1840: A Documentary History*, 3 vols. (New York, 1963). There are also two collections of secondary sources that I recommend: Jacob R. Marcus (ed.), *Critical Studies in American Jewish History* (New York, 1971) 3 volumes, which contains articles from *American Jewish Archives*; and Abraham J.

Karp (ed.), *The Jewish Experience in America* (New York, 1969), 5 volumes, which contains articles from *Publications of the American Jewish Historical Society.*

Many cities and states have had histories of their Jewish populations written, and if some of the older ones are either filiopietistic in tone or antiquarian in emphasis, still they often contain nuggets of information that are unavailable elsewhere. But there are first-rate modern monographs. I particularly recommend the volume by Edwin Wolf and Maxwell Whiteman, *The History of the Jews of Philadelphia from Colonial Times to the Age of Jackson* (Philadelphia, 1957). In the field of biography, as well, the older pietisms have given way to sophisticated analysis. I particularly recommend Jonathan D. Sarna, *Jacksonian Jew: The Two Worlds of Mordecai Noah* (New York, 1981).

More than three decades ago Selig Perlman told my friend, Charles Vevier, in a disparaging remark about the history profession, that it was "the last stronghold of the Anglo-Saxon race." That is no longer true, and it has not been for some time; but the contributions of scholars in the field of late-eighteenth- and nineteenth-century Jewish American history deserve to be better known. The works of Jacob R. Marcus and Bertram W. Korn are classics to those who labor in that vineyard. Korn's *American Jewry and the Civil War* (Philadelphia, 1951) has received wide circulation because the subject is at the epicenter of American history. But how many mainline historians know his equally superb monograph, *The American Reaction to the Mortara Case, 1858–1859* (Cincinnati, 1957), or what the Mortara case was about? The incident is not even mentioned in Ray A. Billington, *The Protestant Crusade, 1800–1860* (New York, 1938). Readers should also consult Korn's *Eventful Years and Experiences: Studies in Nineteenth Century American Jewish History* (Cincinnati, 1959). I have profited enormously from the works of Jacob R. Marcus, who is undoubtedly the dean of American Jewish studies. His *Early American Jewry* (Philadelphia, 1951–53) 2 volumes, and *The Colonial American Jew* (Detroit, 1970) 3 volumes, cover, in the main, an earlier time period; his *Memoirs of American Jews, 1775–1865* (Philadelphia, 1955–56) 3 volumes, is rich and fascinating. In his *Studies in American Jewish History* (Cincinnati, 1969), 17, Marcus calls Isaac Leeser "the hypostasis, the unique essence of nineteenth-century American Jewry, although, in his dynamic urge for accomplishment, he was far ahead of the people he led." I agree.

INDEX